FAITH&
INTELLECT

Leonard J. Arrington

FAITH&
INTELLECT

THE LIVES AND CONTRIBUTIONS
OF LATTER-DAY SAINT THINKERS

LEONARD J. ARRINGTON
FOREWORD BY PHILIP L. BARLOW

EDITED BY GARY JAMES BERGERA

SIGNATURE BOOKS | 2019 | SALT LAKE CITY

The opinions expressed in this book are not necessarily those of the publisher.

Design by Jason Francis.

FIRST EDITION | 2019

LIBRARY OF CONGRESS CATALOGING-IN-PUBLICATION DATA

Names:	Arrington, Leonard J., author. | Bergera, Gary James, editor.
Title:	Faith and intellect : the lives and contributions of Latter-day Saint thinkers / by Leonard J. Arrington.
Description:	First edition. | Salt Lake City : Signature Books, 2019.
Identifiers:	LCCN 2019018833 (print) | LCCN 2019021214 (ebook) | ISBN 9781560853602 (e-book) | ISBN 9781560852759 (pbk. : alk. paper)
Subjects:	LCSH: Mormons—Biography. | Mormon intellectuals—Biography. | Faith and reason. | LCGFT: Biographies.
Classification:	LCC BX8693 (ebook) | LCC BX8693 .A75 2019 (print) | DDC 289.3092/2 [B] —dc23 LC record available at https://lccn.loc.gov/2019018833

CONTENTS

Foreword

PHILIP L. BARLOW

Leonard Arrington was a prophetic figure in the Mormon world of the second half of the twentieth-century.

He was not an institutional prophet, seer, and revelator through apostolic ordination; he was instead a supporter of these. Nor was he, as Joseph Smith's Enoch, a Bible-like prophet, whose fundamental experience was "a communion with the divine consciousness which comes about through the prophet's reflection of, or participation in, the divine pathos."[1] Unlike Nathan and Zechariah, Arrington did not utter, "thus declares the LORD of hosts." He authored no scripture, founded no Zion, made no prognostications by God's authority. Although he exuded a folksy charm and could tell a good story, his prophetic stature did not arise from a compelling charisma and principled eloquence on par with, say, Martin Luther King, who was "just an average-looking fellow, but when he opened his mouth he was like Charlton Heston playing Moses."[2]

It was in a different mode than these that Arrington's voice caught the wind. He was prophetic in that he incarnated something that his fellow Latter-day Saints needed before most of them knew they needed it. He embodied the spirit, values, capacity, credibility, diligence, opportunity, and podium to reclaim and create for them

---

1. This from the phenomenon's most thoughtful analyst, Abraham Heschel, in *The Prophets* (New York: Harper and Row, 1962), 26.

2. Civil rights pioneer Claudette Colvin, qtd. in Brooks Barnes, "From Footnote to Fame in Civil Rights History," *New York Times,* Nov. 25, 2009, at www.nytimes.com/2009/11/26/books/26colvin.html.

a plausible past. He became a "forth teller" (προφήτης?; *prophētēs*) whose telling assumed the guise of informed public candor and balance while grappling with historical issues crucial to LDS identity and faith. So high were the perceived stakes in controlling identity and faith that some church officials, over the objections of others, constricted Arrington's project and ultimately thrust it aside. This act sowed the wind; the Mormon people reaped the whirlwind.

Among other things, the storm yielded a twenty-year chill between the church's administrative and intellectual leaders. In ways that would have pleased Leonard Arrington, the relationship was thawing as the twenty-first century began. A series of shared or parallel initiatives, public church statements issued through official venues, and quiet actions signaled an uneven but important renewed openness and reciprocity.[3]

The earlier permafrost, however, exacted an ongoing toll on a new generation whose native tongue was the internet. This revolutionary forum, democratic without precedent, sometimes hosted competent voices but often partisan, shrill, or ill-informed ones. This cacophonic choir introduced a widening public to versions of the historical and

---

3. The LDS Church History Department in the early decades of the twenty-first century perhaps comprises the flagship of this new openness. The monumental Joseph Smith Papers Project is the most prominent evidence, but the department's enabling of a thorough-going treatment of the Mountain Meadows Massacre and other publishing ventures exceeds the scope and transparency of anything that Arrington was permitted, though the progress would have been implausible without his and his colleagues' efforts decades earlier. Other examples include a series of Gospel Topics essays posted on the church's official website that treat sensitive or controversial issues with more informed candor than previously accessible through official church sources; Apostle M. Russell Ballard's 2016 mandate to the church's seminary and institute teachers that reorients the more constricted and almost century-old philosophy charted by President J. Reuben Clark; efforts to provide more flexibility and authentic discussion in manuals and procedures in Sunday school and other classes; thoughtful statements posted on the church website embracing such matters as the importance of history and the welcoming of new programs of study focusing on Mormonism at secular universities.

social problems that Arrington and his colleagues had earlier attempted to address, with erudition, in the context of faith. The result among an unprepared populace was frequent dismay, even panic, and a sense of betrayal. "Why weren't we told these things while growing up in the church?" The dismay proved contagious among a widening minority, contributing to the Mormon inflection of a growing societal disenchantment with organized religion.[4]

Decades earlier, before becoming a public figure, Arrington had launched his work[5] during an era when the Latter-day Saints were taken seriously by few external scholars, when historical accounts of Mormonism were lobotomized into defending and debunking camps, and when his fellow Saints and their leaders were collectively ambivalent. They were interested, even triumphal, concerning their past, yet some were wary lest too much history erode faith among the innocent. Others hungered for an unvarnished chronicle.

No other person of the twentieth century did more than Arrington to lay grounds for mitigating this unease. It is not that he was the first to write of the Mormon past with courage, relative balance, and sophistication; Juanita Brooks, Russell Mortensen, William Mulder, Dale Morgan, and, despite her own mixed feelings about the church of her youth, Fawn Brodie were among those who preceded

---

4. Jana Riess has conducted an extensive survey of the religious sensibilities of Mormons and former Mormons born in the roughly two decades prior to 2000 (Millennials). Her results show that among those who have left the LDS Church, the five most frequent reasons they cite are that they felt judged or misunderstood, did not trust the church leadership to tell the truth surrounding controversial or historical issues, disagreed with the church's positions on LGBTQ issues, could no longer reconcile their personal values and priorities with those of the church, or simply drifted away from Mormonism. Many others were simply unmoved by church services. Riess, *The Next Mormons: How Millennials Are Changing the LDS Church* (New York: Oxford University Press, 2019). Disengagement from Mormonism is, of course, a particular instance of a wider trend away from organized religion in the United States and elsewhere.

5. Arrington, *Great Basin Kingdom: An Economic History of the Latter-day Saints, 1830–1900* (Cambridge, Massachusetts: Harvard University Press, 1958).

him or began to publish near the same time. Nor was the quality of Arrington's historical scholarship in a class of its own. He enjoyed intellectual peers in such contemporaries as George Ellsworth, Davis Bitton, and Richard Poll and in others only a decade his junior, including Richard Bushman, Jan Shipps, and Armand Mauss. Amidst even this talent, Arrington remained distinctive during his lifetime. Wide ranging in the projects he took on and remarkably prolific, he added to his historical skills a pronounced entrepreneurial outreach—attracting, organizing, enabling, and collaborating with younger scholars around him, becoming their natural leader.

This outreach was formalized—and a Mormon *glastnost* signaled—when in early 1972 Arrington was appointed the first official Historian of the Church of Jesus Christ of Latter-day Saints to be professionally equipped for the task. The widely celebrated appointment, however, also rendered him a public lightning rod for contesting forces within Mormon culture.

As in the wider society—whose coherence during the 1960s and 1970s was tested to the verge of fracture by debate, riot, and more—these contests included matters of race, class, gender, generations, politics, war, education, and social and personal morals. Other prominent figures who enjoined causes related to Arrington's and who remained loyal to the LDS Church were similarly lightning rods for these internal struggles. Examples include Lowell Bennion, Eugene England, and an emerging constellation of LDS feminists such as Claudia Bushman, Laurel Ulrich, and Carol Lynn Pearson. LDS iterations of these cultural tensions added debates over Mormon origins and history.

Given the stresses around such figures and the issues they espoused, and given the reality of change across time and difference across space and class, how ought Latter-day Saints at any given point distinguish the permanent from the transient? Or the transcendent from the mundane? Revelation from policy? Essence from cultural habit? How should believers weigh prophetic authority and personal responsibility in cases where they seem at odds? One quandary undergirds the others: In a Mormon context that respects revelation and ecclesiastical authority, what is the proper relationship between faith and intellect?

In May 1993, LDS Apostle Boyd K. Packer shared his influential perspective on this question by including intellectuals, or a certain class of them ("so-called intellectuals"), as one LDS group which had been "caught up and led away by social and political unrest" and which presented a danger, having "made major invasions into the membership of the Church."[6] Four months later tensions deepened when six LDS intellectuals in disparate locations and of different dispositons were concurrently excommunicated, an event interpreted as a shot across the bow of the intellectual community and widely reported in American media and beyond. Perhaps influenced by such swirls, the History Department at BYU–Hawaii promptly inaugurated a series on "Faith and Intellect," inviting Leonard Arrington to be the first annual lecturer for the following year (1994). The resulting four lectures form the core of the book you are about to read, supplemented by additional material, as editor Gary James Bergera explains.

Arrington was persuaded that an adequate reckoning of LDS faith in relation to the intellect required a historical perspective. He did not attempt a history of how Mormon authorities and culture had regarded the life of the mind as a whole, as this would have required a narrative of competing strands of indifference and anti-intellectualism, as well as regard for the mind.[7] Rather, he sought to establish in the Mormon past the compatibility of faith and intellect.

---

6. "Talk to the All-Church Coordinating Council," May 18, 1993, at www.zionsbest.com/face.html.

7. Cf. Philip Barlow, "Mind and Spirit in Mormon Thought," *Oxford Handbook of Mormonism* (New York: Oxford University Press, 2015), 227–45.

He articulated this tradition not through doctrinal exposition or philosophical postulates, but through biography. In Goethe's terms:

> Listen, my friend: the golden tree
> Of life is green, all theory is grey.[8]

The lives and accomplishments of the women and men through whom Arrington sketched this tradition ranged from the movement's prophetic founder to Arrington's own contemporaries (some of whom are still alive a quarter-century later) who drew strength from both mind and spirit as they navigated the currents of human experience. He anticipated that his choices might be questioned. Was Joseph Smith an "intellectual" as the subtitle of chapter 1 asserts? Was Brigham Young? (chapter 2). The reader must draw her own conclusions as Arrington explains and defends his selected subjects. And because the term "intellectual" is had for good and evil among virtually all nations, kindreds, tongues, and peoples, the broad but careful definition Arrington crafts in his Introduction invites scrutiny.

The chapters that follow are not only biographical toward their respective subjects, but also collectively and implicitly autobiographical in relation to their author. They open a portal into what Arrington himself valued in life and in religion. To him, Chieko Okazaki, Emmeline Wells, James Talmage, Henry Eyring, and the others were heroic Saints. They are models of "intellectual vitality, spiritual power, and moral courage." They encountered obstacles and their responses appeal to "the better angels of our nature."

This self-revealing dimension of Arrington's mind—what he esteemed—haunts the book: its conception and structure, its

---

8. John R. Williams, trans., *Faust, A Tragedy,* in *The Essential Goethe: John Wolfgang von Goethe,* ed. Matthew Bell (Princeton: Princeton University Press, 2016), 298, lines 2038–39. Approaching Mormon history through collected, abbreviated biography was also his strategy in *Mormons and Their Historians,* co-authored with Davis Bitton (Salt Lake City: University of Utah Press, 1988), and *The Presidents of the Church* (Salt Lake City: Deseret Book Co., 1986).

concerns and values, its selections and omissions, its motives and conclusions. His own life looms between the lines of the whole, comprising an additional chapter, *passim,* not listed in the Table of Contents. This invisible chapter is fitting, for Leonard Arrington became an oracle to the Mormon people not merely by what he said, but also by what he was: a stubbornly optimistic man of intelligence and faith. He insisted that critical thought need not grow spiritually inert, and that faith need not remain naïve.

Editor's Preface

In late 1993, Leonard J. Arrington (b. 1917), former official Historian of the LDS Church, was invited by the history department at Brigham Young University–Hawaii to deliver the first set of lectures in a newly inaugurated series on "Faith and Intellect" the next year. Arrington would be followed in future years by prominent Catholic, Protestant, and other religions' historians.

Arrington began working on the project immediately and presented four lectures—what are now chapters 1, 2, 3, and 7—in May 1994 treating some prominent nineteenth- and twentieth-century LDS intellectuals. When he subsequently decided to produce a book on the subject, he prepared three additional chapters (4, 5, and 6), an introduction, and a conclusion. While focusing on well-known LDS Church members, Arrington included at the end of the chapters briefer mention of some of his subjects' contemporaries.

Arrington conceived the purpose of the book as sketching the lives and contributions of Latter-day Saints who possessed both faith and intellect. While he delineated some of the tensions and resolutions involving faith and intellect at various stages of LDS history, he emphasized men and women who confronted the challenges of thought and experience in the light of the church's belief in continuing heavenly revelation.

In his preface, Arrington expressed his appreciation as follows: "I am grateful to the administrators and professors of history, literature, science, and religion at BYU–Hawaii who made helpful comments; and to two friends in Salt Lake City who read and improved the manuscript: Heidi Swinton and Davis Bitton. I am grateful to my wife, Harriet, who typed the manuscript into her computer. Above all, I am indebted to scholars who prepared the papers, articles, and books mentioned in the notes that have been helpful in making this book as informative and accurate as possible. For errors of omission and commission, I assume all responsibility."

Of the documentary sources he cited and quoted, Arrington sometimes made minor adjustments to punctuation, capitalization, tense, etc., but was careful not to change the meaning of any.

More than a decade after Arrington's death in 1999, I was invited by his family to prepare an edition of his diaries for publication. While working on that project, I discovered his "Faith and Intellect" manuscript among his papers, and asked the Arrington family if they would consent to its publication. They agreed, and I began work on it after completing the diaries manuscript.

In editing "Faith and Intellect," I made what corrections and adjustments I believe benefit Arrington's intentions as well as the manuscript's readability, organization, and presentation. This includes, among other minor changes, silently updating some of his footnotes. I approached Arrington's work as I would any manuscript submitted by a living author for publication. Arrington wanted his book to celebrate the integration of faith and intellect as manifested in the lives of high-profile LDS Church members whom he respected and admired. While not ignoring the difficulties, Arrington intentionally stressed the positive. For Arrington, intellectual curiosity and inquiry could lead to greater spirituality. He hoped, in this book, to convey a sense of the value an intellectually informed approach to the LDS Church and its teachings had been for him in his own life.

Introduction

Throughout the history of the Church of Jesus Christ of Latter-day Saints, its leaders and apologists have declared that faith and intellect enjoy a mutually supportive relationship. Faith opens the way to knowledge, and knowledge reaches up to reverence. Spiritual understanding comes with faith and is supported by intellect. As LDS Church President Spencer W. Kimball told Brigham Young University students in 1976: "As LDS scholars, you must speak with authority and excellence to your professional colleagues in the language of scholarship, and you must also be literate in the language of spiritual things."[1]

The theme of faith *and* intellect, not faith *versus* intellect, was established in the early days of the Mormon Restoration. Founding Church Prophet Joseph Smith taught that "it is impossible for a man to be saved in ignorance" (D&C 131:6), and that "a man is saved no faster than he gets knowledge."[2] "If a person gains more knowledge and intelligence in this life through his diligence and obedience than another, he will have so much the advantage in the world to come" (D&C 130:19). "Seek ye out of the best books words of wisdom, seek learning even by study and by faith," for "the glory of God is intelligence, or, in other words, light and truth" (D&C 109:7, 93:36). In a revelation to Smith in 1829, his

---

1. Spencer W. Kimball, "Second Century Address," *BYU Studies* 16 (Summer 1976): 466.
2. Joseph Fielding Smith, ed., *Teachings of the Prophet Joseph Smith* (Salt Lake City: Deseret Book Co., 1976), 217.

colleague Oliver Cowdery was instructed that spiritual insight is not a product of the "heart" only. The use of the intellect could not be ignored in seeking the revealed word (D&C 8 and 9).[3] Indeed Smith's visions and revelations initiated "a dynamic interplay between mind and spirit."[4]

Intellectual activity has been the means of developing and enriching life and faith among the Latter-day Saints and furthering the growth and betterment of the kingdom of God.[5] LDS theology reaches for a balance between rationalistic explanations and transcendental impressions.

The belief that intellectual activity is an aspect of worship was built upon the teachings of Jesus, who insisted upon the harmony of faith and intellect: "Thou shalt love the Lord thy God with all thy heart, and with all thy soul, and with all thy mind" (Matt. 22:37). There is a similar statement in Section 4 of the Doctrine and Covenants: "See that ye serve him [God] with all your heart, might, mind and strength" (v. 2). Under these instructions, Latter-day Saints sought knowledge out of the best books (see D&C 88:118) and established schools for instruction in both sacred and secular matters. These began with the Schools of the Prophets in Ohio and in Missouri and continued on the western frontier with the establishment of LDS ward schools, stake academies, colleges, and universities.

Faith means trust in God, in the gospel, in fellow church members, and in life—a confidence that the world is God's and that when the gospel dwells among us, and we teach and instruct one another with the wisdom in the best books, we will have the spirit of Christ (Col. 3:16). Far from being the antithesis of faith, intellect

---

3. See also Mark R. Grandstaff, "Having More Learning Than Sense," *Dialogue: A Journal of Mormon Thought* 26 (Winter 1993): 41.

4. Richard F. Haglund Jr. and David J. Whittaker, "Intellectual History," in *Encyclopedia of Mormonism*, 4 vols. (New York: Macmillan, 1992), 2:687.

5. Ibid., 685. There may, of course, have been instances in which intellectual activity has had an opposite effect.

helps us express our wonderment and enthusiasm in creative, meaningful ways, ways that may awaken a sense of gratitude and awe.[6]

The men and women I discuss in rough chronological order in the following chapters were persons of both intellect and faith. One might think of them as representing five stages of LDS intellectual history:[7] the restoration period, 1830–44 (chapter 1); the pioneer church, 1847–90 (chapters 2 and 3); the church and the "New Learning," 1891–1945 (chapters 4 and 5); and the modern church (chapters 6 and 7). Each chapter focuses on one or more personality, who, in representing the thought and faith of the period, faced challenges in their thinking and leadership. This discussion is supplemented with brief accounts of other leaders of that time who also faced challenges of faith and intellect. The emphasis is not on the principal confrontations of faith and intellect, although these are mentioned, but on the lives of the persons discussed and the manner in which they exhibited the harmony of faith and intellect as taught by latter-day scripture.

Many of those mentioned in these chapters are, or would not mind being regarded as, intellectuals. A few of them might not recognize or would even look askance at the term. "Intellectuals are persons of superior intelligence—persons devoted to matters of the mind whether in the arts and letters, science, or theology; persons given to study, reflection, and speculation, especially concerning large, profound, or abstract issues; persons engaged in activity requiring preeminently the use of intellect."[8] They are usually viewed as persons who are capable of commenting upon society and its problems "with greater detachment than those more directly caught up in the practical business of production and power."[9]

---

6. Van Austin Harvey, *The Historian and the Believer: The Morality of Historical Knowledge and Christian Belief* (New York: Macmillan, 1966), 264.

7. Haglund and Whittaker, "Intellectual History," 2:685–91, for a similar listing.

8. See *Webster's New International Dictionary,* s.v., "Intellectual."

9. Christopher Lasch, *The New Radicalism in America, 1889–1963: The Intellectual as a Social Type* (New York: Alfred A. Knopf, 1965), ix.

There is a special problem involved in seeking to denote intellectuals in a religious group as fully committed as the Latter-day Saints. A "real intellectual," it is sometimes said, does not subordinate rationalism to other ways of knowing, such as authoritarianism or spiritual intuition.[10] But, it is said, "good Mormons" do, for that is a part of their mortal probation. On the other hand, it is said that LDS intellectuals rationalize that revelation is superior to reason. My experience is that serious Latter-day Saints regard faith and intellect as complements, not as competitors.

Dictionary and encyclopedia definitions of "intellectual" permit the inclusion of persons with religious faith. There is no definition that would disqualify St. Augustine, Thomas Aquinas, Thomas More, Cardinal John Henry Newman, or, for that matter, Joseph Smith and some of those who accepted his revelations. No one, I think, would disqualify any Latter-day Saint leader of thought because of any narrow definition.[11]

Some persons might contend that my inclusion of a chapter on Brigham Young is an undue broadening of the term "intellectual." Young was certainly not an intellectual in any narrow definition of the term, but I include him because he was a person of intellectual

---

10. The word "authoritarian" refers to subjection to authority—an undesirable state; "authoritative" means sanctioned by authority and is usually regarded as something desirable. Lowell Bennion cautions that Mormonism is authoritative but not authoritarian. Bennion, *Religion and the Pursuit of Truth* (Salt Lake City: Deseret Book Co., 1959), 24–29.

11. Penetrating essays that discuss Mormonism and intellectuals are Ephraim E. Ericksen, "William H. Chamberlin, Pioneer Mormon Philosopher," *Western Humanities Review* 8 (Autumn 1954): 275–85; R. Kent Fielding, "Historical Perspectives for a Liberal Mormonism," *Western Humanities Review* 14 (Winter 1960): 69–80; Davis Bitton, "Anti-Intellectualism in Mormon History," *Dialogue: A Journal of Mormon Thought* 1 (Autumn 1966), 111–34 (also the "Comment" of James B. Allen on 134–40); and Thomas F. O'Dea, "Sources of Strain and Conflict," in *The Mormons* (Chicago: University of Chicago Press, 1957), 222–57. See also Charles R. Harrell, *"This Is My Doctrine": The Development of Mormon Theology* (Salt Lake City: Greg Kofford Books, 2011).

power and mental alertness, and had enormous influence on his generation of Saints—influence on doctrine, on "practical" thought, on the images and metaphors that have become part of the gospel. He helped to found Brigham Young Academy, Brigham Young College, and the University of Deseret, which educated intellectuals like B. H. Roberts, James E. Talmage, John A. Widtsoe, William H. Chamberlain, Ephraim E. Ericksen, and others.

The primary question of intellectuality is the extent to which one's emotional attachment to certain "final truths" informs her intellectual pursuit, whether her soul-searching prevents her thought on key issues from being freely detachable from her own cultural traditions. Noted British philosopher Bertrand Russell suggests that in studying a given philosopher or line of thought "the right attitude is neither reverence nor contempt, but first a kind of hypothetical sympathy." One should cultivate the enlargement of the scope of her mind beyond her own "cherished prejudices" by exercising her historical and psychological imagination.[12] There would seem to be no inherent reason why our more sophisticated thinkers could not thus project their minds as have highly committed persons in other religions and cultures.

American intellectual historian Richard Hofstadter posits two qualities in the intellectual's attitude toward ideas—playfulness and piety. Playfulness, he writes, is openness to the potential of ideas—"sheer delight in intellectual activity" in the quest for new uncertainties. The other quality is piety, for the intellectual recognizes that values underlie every question that is posed; the life of the mind has a "kind of primary moral significance. ... The intellectual is *engagé*—he is pledged, committed, enlisted. What everyone else

---

12. Bertrand Russell, *A History of Western Philosophy* (New York: Simon and Schuster, 1945), 39.

is willing to admit, namely that ideas and abstractions are of signal importance in human life, he imperatively feels."[13]

How open and engaged have Latter-day Saint men and women been in searching for truth? How creative and playful have they been in developing new interpretations and hypotheses? With respect to the luminaries described in these chapters, what has been the relationship between their minds and their testimonies? Granted that each has been influenced by "the best thinking of men," how has that affected their faith? To put it the other way around, has the inspiration of "revealed truths" strengthened or weakened their reasoning? If one's knowledge or assurance of the truth of the Lord's work comes from reason, or logic, or persuasive argument, can it lead to a testimony of the gospel without revelation? Do the lives and works of some of those described in this book provide supporting affirmative evidence? When Jesus said, "Ye shall know the truth and the truth shall make you free" (John 8:32), did he have in mind only spiritual truth, or reasoned truth as well?

These essays are written in the historical tradition of exemplary lives. I try to give a vision of greatness in both intellect and faith among selected LDS leaders. The men and women described are human beings, with observable imperfections, but they exhibited, I believe, intellectual vitality, spiritual power, and moral courage, and appealed to "the better angels of our nature." God's spirit shone through their writings and actions. I try to acknowledge reality, but in my judgment, the persons I discuss are worthy heroes and heroines. For each of them, faith and intellect were partners. Or, to use the analogy of Socrates in Plato's *Phaedrus,* the human soul, like a charioteer, must drive two horses as it progresses toward heaven. The horses must work together or the chariot will just go round

---

13. Richard Hofstadter, *Anti-Intellectualism in American Life* (New York: Alfred A. Knopf, 1963), 27–30.

and round.[14] To St. Augustine, the horses might be spirit and flesh; to Shakespeare, passion and reason; and for our purposes, faith and intellect. It would be unfortunate if either should outstretch the other. Emphasizing intellect would neglect spirituality, emphasizing faith might produce mediocrity, fanaticism, or intolerance. We cannot achieve spiritual excellence without intellectual rigor, and intellectual excellence is hollow without active spirituality. We need to have the Spirit as we learn, and we need to have learning as we build faith. Working together, faith and intellect may help us achieve the Latter-day Saint goal of eternal progression.

---

14. See B. Jowett, *The Works of Plato,* four volumes in one (New York: Dial Press, 1938), 3:361–449 ("Phaedrus"); and Neal W. Kramer, "The Intellect and the Spirit," *New Perspectives* 9 (December 1992): 14–20.

CHAPTER 1

Joseph Smith

INTELLECTUAL AND MAN OF THE PEOPLE

Joseph Smith (1805–44), founding prophet of the Church of Jesus Christ of Latter-day Saints, was a man of intellect and charm, remembered especially by believers for his revelations, sociability, and personality.[1] Visionary, city-planner, candidate for president of the United States, and father of eleven children (of whom two were adopted), he was also an imaginative organizer, friend of the helpless, effective debater, and student of the scriptures. In an era when religious revivalism was characterized by intense enthusiasm, preachers pounding the pulpit demanding fealty and fear of God, Smith spoke of ideas and images, expanded perspectives of a largely uneducated people, and respected the commentary of others. He was at home, whether discussing religious philosophies or playing a

---

1. Full-length biographies of Smith include John Henry Evans, *Joseph Smith: An American Prophet* (New York: Macmillan, 1933, reprinted by Deseret Book Co. in 1989); Donna Hill, *Joseph Smith: The First Mormon* (Garden City, New York: Doubleday & Co., 1977); Richard L. Bushman, *Joseph Smith and the Beginnings of Mormonism* (Urbana: University of Illinois Press, 1984); Larry C. Porter and Susan Easton Black, eds., *The Prophet Joseph: Essays on the Life and Mission of Joseph Smith* (Salt Lake City: Deseret Book Co., 1988); and Richard Lyman Bushman, *Joseph Smith: Rough Stone Rolling* (New York: Alfred A. Knopf, 2005). For more detailed treatments, see Dan Vogel, *Joseph Smith: The Making of a Prophet* (Salt Lake City: Signature Books, 2004); Richard S. Van Wagoner, *Natural Born Seer: Joseph Smith, American Prophet, 1805–1830* (Salt Lake City: Smith–Pettit Foundation, 2016); and Martha Bradley-Evans, *Glorious in Persecution: Joseph Smith, American Prophet, 1839–1844* (Salt Lake City: Smith–Pettit Foundation, 2016).

game of ball with a group of boys. He walked the streets of Nauvoo, Illinois, during the early to mid-1840s, played with children, chatted with neighbors, and opened his home to every kind of visitor. I see him as the sort of person whom the Lord would choose to restore his church.

Although not schooled or well read by traditional standards, Smith was a person with both intellectual powers and charisma. John M. Bernhisel, graduate of the Philadelphia Medical School and Utah's first (and four-term) delegate to the US Congress, an LDS convert who was a physician for the Saints in Nauvoo, lived for most of a year with Smith and his wife, Emma Hale Smith. Just before Smith's death in June 1844, Bernhisel gave this appraisal of his friend:

> Joseph Smith is naturally a man of strong mental powers, and is possessed of much energy and decision of character, great penetration, and a profound knowledge of human nature—He is a man of calm judgment, enlarged views, and is eminently distinguished by his love of justice. He is kind and obliging, generous and benevolent, sociable and cheerful, and is possessed of a mind of a contemplative and reflective character; he is honest, frank, fearless, and independent, and as free from dissimulation as any man to be found. But it is in the gentle charities of domestic life, as the tender and affectionate husband & parent, the warm and sympathizing friend, that the prominent traits of his character are revealed.[2]

Here is a similar appraisal by Emmeline B. Wells who, as a well-educated girl of fourteen, left Massachusetts and joined the Latter-day Saints in Nauvoo in the spring of 1844:

> In the Prophet Joseph Smith, I believed I recognized the great spiritual power that brought joy and comfort to the Saints; and withal

---

2. John M. Bernhisel to Thomas Ford, June 14, 1844, Joseph Smith's Office Papers, 1835–1844, Church History Library, Church of Jesus Christ of Latter-day Saints, Salt Lake City, Utah, hereafter LDS Church History Library.

he had that strong comradeship that made such a bond of brotherliness with those who were his companions in civil and military life, and in which he reached men's souls, and appealed most forcibly to their friendship and loyalty. He possessed too the innate refinement that one finds in the born poet, or in the most highly cultivated intellectual and poetical nature.[3]

Not a systematic theologian, Smith was a syncretic revelator—he made known teachings that he believed had been revealed to him by heavenly manifestations and in dreams and visions. He communicated these to followers in books of scripture, articles in church periodicals, and sermons. The products of his mental and revelatory powers included the Book of Mormon and the Book of Abraham; the Book of Moses, an explication and emendation of the text of the Old and New Testaments; modern revelations published in the Book of Commandments and Doctrine and Covenants; doctrinal instructions; and comments about such texts as the Apocrypha and Pseudepigrapha. Above all, with his introduction of new scriptures and revelations, he demonstrated the limitations of Bible literalism which circumscribed the religious doctrines and practices of the Protestants of his day.[4] His thoughts and expressions challenged and revised many widely held doctrines. Yet, for his followers, he was convincing as a pulpit orator and presenter of ideas, well conceived and expounded.

Men and women, Smith taught, are eternal beings, children of heavenly parents. As part of an eternal plan, men and women are on Earth to be tested by good and evil and progress toward becoming

---

3. Emmeline B. Wells, Statement in "Joseph Smith, The Prophet," *Young Woman's Journal* 16 (December 1905): 556.

4. Much of Smith's thought is contained in Joseph Fielding Smith, ed., *Teachings of the Prophet Joseph Smith* (Salt Lake City: Deseret News, 1938); and Andrew F. Ehat and Lyndon W. Cook, eds., *The Words of Joseph Smith* (Provo, Utah: BYU Religious Studies Center, 1980). Also important is the Joseph Smith Papers Project, with volumes published by the LDS Church Historian's Press, Salt Lake City.

Joseph Smith

gods and goddesses when they return to Heaven for eternity. Saints make progress toward this goal by obeying the principles of the gospel and receiving all the ordinances of salvation, including those performed in the LDS temple, where Earth meets Heaven and eternal relationships are formed by covenants.

Smith became concerned about religion when he was about age twelve, if not earlier; he read the scriptures, prayed, had discussions with his father and mother, and attended a variety of religious services. He also joined a debating society.

In his adolescence, he later said, he knelt in a clearing in some nearby woods and began to pray. He was "filled with the spirit of God," and had the experience Latter-day Saints have come to refer to as the First Vision, a manifestation of the Father and Son. In the years that followed, he went about his mundane duties with his family, clearing and fencing land, planting trees and crops, and working nearby farms. His instruction by his mother and father in reading, writing, and arithmetic continued. In 1823, Smith later said, he was visited by a heavenly messenger who informed him that he would be given a mission to translate some sacred plates left by former inhabitants of the American continent, and thus provide a new testimony of Jesus Christ and his teachings.

In his 1832 description of his early visionary experience, Smith revealed that he had been torn between the universalism and rationalism of his father's beliefs and his mother's emphasis on the spiritual quality of religion. Here was the conflict between faith and intellect that Smith prayed about, which heavenly revelation helped him to resolve. Thus, through his father, Smith inherited the rationalism of the Enlightenment and the philosophical movement of the seventeenth and eighteenth centuries that stressed the power of human reason and worked for improvements in politics, religion, and education. From his mother, he inherited the enthusiasm and religious excitement and warmth, zeal, and ardor of contemporary New England. One gets true religion "by study and by faith"; "the mind and the heart" (D&C 9:8; also 8:2). On the one hand, Smith seemed not to have feared intellectual inquiry; on the other hand, he mostly welcomed "gifts of the spirit," such as faith healing, speaking in tongues, and shouts of "Hosanna" at the dedication of temples.

For Smith, Christ's gospel includes all truth—scientific and religious. Matter is neither created nor destroyed; God organized the elements when he "created" the earth. Our spirits are eternal, uncreated entities, and exist under the universal law governing free and partially equal beings. Jesus taught the plan of salvation leading toward our potential of exaltation or "fullness of joy." Joy comes from growth and overcoming problems. Gospel principles help men and women achieve a better pattern of life. All things are spiritual, including principles of economics, sociology, politics, and all the sciences.

Smith's failure to develop a systematic, comprehensive theology was, of course, partly due to the opposition he encountered throughout his career and partly to his lack of formal education. Smith was no Thomas Aquinas, the thirteenth-century Catholic philosopher whose *Summa Theologica* gave a carefully organized and precise analysis of God, his attributes, and his relation to the universe. Nevertheless, Smith's teachings provided answers to questions of human existence; he was a prophet to his people, a conveyor of the will of deity. His sermons, according to those who heard them, were intellectually and spiritually uplifting and satisfying. Smith's so-called King Follett discourse, given before 8,000 men and women in Nauvoo in April 1844, is still regarded by Latter-day Saints as one of his greatest sermons. In this last general conference address delivered less than three months before he was killed, Smith discussed the character of God, the origin and destiny of humankind, the unpardonable sin, the resurrection of children, the Creation, the tie between the living and their progenitors, and his love for all men and women.[5] British immigrant Joseph Fielding, who was present at the two-hour oration, wrote: "It is the voice of a god, not of a man."[6]

Smith esteemed almost all people, enjoyed life, loved to hear friends sing, had a tender heart, was a confident leader of a wide diversity of people, and a great preacher. As contemporary Wandle Mace wrote, "I do know that no man could explain the scriptures—throw them wide open to view so plain that none could misunderstand their meaning—except he had been taught of God [as had Joseph Smith]."[7]

---

5. Donald Q. Cannon, "The King Follett Discourse: Joseph Smith's Greatest Sermon in Historical Perspective," *BYU Studies* 18 (Winter 1978): 186, 179–92. In the same issue of *BYU Studies* are Van Hale, "The Doctrinal Impact of the King Follett Discourse," 209–25, and Stanley Larson, "The King Follett Discourse: A Newly Amalgamated Text," 193–208.

6. Copy in my files.

7. Autobiography of Wandle Mace, typescript, 22, Special Collections, J. Willard Marriott Library, University of Utah, Salt Lake City.

Much was made of this skill by Brigham Young, who boasted that he knew Smith as well as any man:

> The excellency of the glory of the character of brother Joseph Smith was that he could reduce heavenly things to the understanding of the finite. When he preached to the people—revealed the things of God, the will of God, the plan of salvation, the purposes of Jehovah, the relation in which we stand to him and all the heavenly beings, he reduced his teachings to the capacity of every man, woman, and child, making them as plain as a well-defined pathway. This should have convinced every person that ever heard of him of his divine authority and power, for no other man was able to teach as he could, and no person can reveal the things of God, but by the revelations of Jesus. When we hear a man that can speak of heavenly things, and present them to the people in a way that they can be understood, you may know that to that man the avenue is open, and that he, by some power, has communication with heavenly beings; and when the highest intelligence is exhibited, he, perhaps, has communication with the highest intelligence that exists.[8]

A major problem facing Smith came to a head in 1838 when several members of the Quorum of Twelve Apostles, organized only three years earlier, refused to support his Kingdom-oriented goals and left the church. Smith had published in the 1835 first edition of the Doctrine and Covenants a statement on government that emphasized freedom of religion, freedom of opinion, and the need for government to be free from the influence of any particular religion. Nevertheless, the Saints tended to follow their leaders on economic and political matters and were group-oriented. There were disagreements and misunderstandings among leaders about specific policies and doctrines and about styles of leadership. What was the proper

---

8. Brigham Young, Sermon of October 14, 1860, *Journal of Discourses,* 26 vols. (Liverpool, England: Latter-day Saints Booksellers Depot, 1854–86), 8:206 (hereafter JD).

role of the church? To what extent should the church dictate use of property, voting patterns, and control over individual lives?

In February 1838, the presidency of the church in Missouri—David Whitmer, W. W. Phelps, and John Whitmer—were tried by a church council and released. On April 7, charges were launched against Oliver Cowdery, associate president of the church, whose desire for personal financial independence ran counter to the cooperative economics essential to the Zion society that Smith envisioned. Asserting that the church could not exercise that degree of temporal autonomy over him, Cowdery was excommunicated. The high council also dropped from membership Lyman Johnson, one of the Twelve Apostles. These actions took two of the three witnesses to the Book of Mormon (Cowdery and Whitmer) and one of the apostles (Johnson). Within a year, three other apostles were excommunicated. It was a time of tension, from within and without.[9] Clearly, some leaders as well as followers were disturbed by the increased direction church leaders gave members in temporal matters and by Smith's involvement in economic affairs. Some preferred the less complicated faith they had embraced in the church's infancy.

In an attempt to get the measure of the man, I would like to summarize the impressions of perhaps 200 men and women, all church members, who knew Smith personally and left accounts of their experiences with him in diaries, letters, recollections, autobiographies, talks, or in one of the LDS Church magazines: *Juvenile Instructor, Young Woman's Journal, Woman's Exponent, Millennial Star.* These first-person accounts are by those who believed Smith had visions, received revelations, and was given, line upon line, the plan of salvation, the framework of church organization, and the latter-day record

---

9. See James B. Allen and Glen M. Leonard, *The Story of the Latter-day Saints,* 2nd ed. (Salt Lake City: Deseret Book Co., 1992), 104, 129–30; Richard Lloyd Anderson, "Oliver Cowdery," in *Encyclopedia of Mormonism,* 4 vols., ed. Daniel H. Ludlow (New York: Macmillan, 1992), 1:335–40.

of instructions that became the Doctrine and Covenants. I realize that one must be careful in accepting all of these accounts at face value. But when any of them are first hand, consistent with the rest of what is known about Smith, and corroborated from other sources, I believe they can provide dependable evidences of Smith's human qualities. Their impressions may be summarized as follows:

1. Smith loved people—old people, young people, children, and babies; intellectuals and the unschooled; the scholarly and the village roustabouts; farmers, mechanics, bankers, housewives, and professors. He felt deeply about someone's problems and sometimes wept when he heard of someone being mistreated or in intense pain from an accident or illness.

2. Usually well dressed, Smith was outgoing, convivial, and full of life. He was sociable, enjoyed dancing and good food, often taking popcorn with sugar and cream in the evenings, and sometimes joining a group in singing hymns and popular songs. At dinners and parties, he often joined in the dishwashing and cleaning up. He was caught on one occasion with holes in the elbows of his jacket, but he was not embarrassed and not too proud to give a sermon thus attired.[10] In social relations, he considered everyone his equal. People liked to be with him. He enjoyed the theater, circus performances, and excursions on the Mississippi River, which bordered Nauvoo.

3. For the times in which he lived, Smith had a surprisingly enlightened view of the place of women. As described by Orson F. Whitney, an apostle and historian—and grandson of church leaders Heber C. Kimball and Newel K. Whitney—Smith taught:

> … the sisters were to act with the brethren, to stand side by side with them, and to enjoy the benefits and blessings of the priesthood, the delegated authority of God.

---

10. "History of Goudy Hogan from His Own Diary," typescript, 6, 53, Special Collections, Merrill-Cazier Library, Utah State University, Logan.

The lifting of the women of Zion to that plane was the beginning of a work for the elevation of womankind through[out] the world. ... The turning of the key by the Prophet of God, and the setting up in this Church, of women's organizations, [were] signs of a new era, one of those sunbursts of light that proclaim the dawning of a new dispensation.[11]

4. Smith was evidently something of an athlete. Organized athletics were not part of the scene in those early days, but Smith enjoyed spontaneous "sports": ice skating, hiking, ball games, woodcutting, and building log cabins. As one oldtimer told an audience of young people in Enterprise, Utah, in 1908: "I have seen him wrestle with the young men on the green. He was quick as a squirrel and strong as a mountain lion."[12]

5. Smith enjoyed word games, homemade poetry and doggerel, limericks, rebuses (stories with drawn pictures in place of words), and comic verse. He was also, according to Daniel H. Wells, a non-Mormon business and civic official in Commerce (later Nauvoo), "the best lawyer I have ever known in all my life."[13]

6. Smith was courageous, bold-spirited, gallant, and fearless. His leadership was especially noteworthy as he directed the 200 men who marched in 1834 from Ohio to Missouri to help the Saints there. As George A. Smith, a cousin and later LDS apostle, wrote:

The Prophet ... never uttered a murmur or complaint, while most of the men in the camp complained to him of sore toes, blistered feet, long drives, scanty supply of provisions, poor quality of bread, bad corn dodger [i.e., corn-meal cake or dumpling], "frouzey" [i.e.,

11. Orson F. Whitney, "Woman's Work and 'Mormonism,'" *Young Woman's Journal* 17 (July 1906): 293–95.

12. Lyman L. Woods, qtd. in Nels Anderson, *Desert Saints: The Mormon Frontier in Utah* (Chicago: University of Chicago Press, 1942), 5.

13. *Journal of Jesse Nathaniel Smith* (Salt Lake City: Smith Family Association, 1951), 455–56.

foul-smelling] butter, strong honey, maggoty bacon and cheese, etc. Even a dog could not bark at some men without their murmuring at Joseph. If they had to camp with bad water, it would nearly cause rebellion. Yet we were the Camp of Zion, and many of us were careless, thoughtless, heedless, foolish or devilish, and yet we did not know it. Joseph had to bear with us and tutor us like children.[14]

Years later, Brigham Young reflected on the impression of the long march: "I told those brethren that I was well-paid—paid with heavy interest—yea, that my measure was filled to overflowing with the knowledge that I had received by traveling with the Prophet."[15]

In 1892, aware that many of the persons who knew Smith were beginning to die—almost fifty years had passed since his death—George Q. Cannon, editor of the monthly 32-page *Juvenile Instructor,* used in LDS Sunday schools, urged those with personal memories of Smith to record and submit them for publication. During the year 1892, twenty-one men and seven women submitted accounts that were published under the general heading "Recollections of Joseph Smith." The incidents revealed a man of spiritual power whose earthly experiences focused on his physical strength, his kindness and warmth to children, his cheery nature, and his escapes from persecution.

In December 1905, on the occasion of the 100th anniversary of Smith's birth, the *Young Woman's Journal,* edited by Susa Young Gates, published the accounts of ten women who were still alive and had known him, under the heading "Joseph Smith, the Prophet." To these were added, the following December, the stories of five women and three men. Almost thirty years later, Edwin F. Parry, director of Deseret Book Company and a member of the Church's General Sunday School Board, published fifty-seven accounts in *Stories*

---

14. George A. Smith, "Memoirs," June 25, 1834, in George A. Smith Papers, 1834–1877, LDS Church History Library.

15. Brigham Young, Sermon, October 6, 1862, in JD 10:20.

About Joseph Smith the Prophet (Salt Lake City, 1934).[16] Finally, there are stories of surviving "Old Nauvooers" told to twentieth-century audiences and remembered by some still alive. Twentieth-century LDS Church educator T. Edgar Lyon, who grew up in an area of Salt Lake City in which many Old Nauvooers resided, reported:

> Month after month I heard such incidents related—how Joseph Smith visited unannounced in the homes, had children sit on his lap as he told them stories, admonished them to be honest, to love and obey their parents, not to quarrel with each other, and to be helpful to those who were sick or in need. They related his eagerness to arm wrestle, pull sticks, or participate in other contemporary games of physical prowess. They recalled how "The Prophet" dropped by their homes at mealtime, ate with the family, and kept a lively conversation going, or how some of them had been guests at his table with Emma Smith as hostess.[17]

In my own study of Mormon history, I have accumulated a file of additional first-person accounts of Smith, published and unpublished, so that we now have perhaps 200 first-hand stories of personal experiences and impressions. The accounts offer a rare glimpse into the unofficial life of the LDS Church and its prophet, especially in the late 1830s and 1840s. A few of these follow as examples.

The first is that of William Taylor, younger brother of Apostle (later President) John Taylor. Hounded, Joseph and John Taylor in October 1842 spent a couple of weeks out of sight in Quawka, a day's walk from Nauvoo, at the cabin home of Taylor's parents, James and Agnes Taylor. Smith stayed three weeks, and enjoyed

---

16. Many of these and some others were published by Hyrum L. Andrus and Helen Mae Andrus in *They Knew the Prophet* (Salt Lake City: Bookcraft, 1974).

17. T. Edgar Lyon, "Recollections of 'Old Nauvooers': Memories from Oral History," *BYU Studies* 18 (Winter 1978): 143–50, which tells stories Lyon heard as a boy and young man in meetings in the old LDS Twentieth Ward chapel in the early years of the twentieth century.

the potato pies, roast lamb, and Cumbrian sauce. Most of the days he went tramping through the woods with the Taylors' nineteen-year-old son, William. The two men, one seventeen years younger than the other, were delighted when they sighted squirrels, pigeons, ducks, and other forest life. William remembered that they did not encounter any person on these hikes. Recalling these days with Smith, William said:

> I have never known the same joy and satisfaction in the companionship of any other person, man or woman, that I felt with him, the man who had conversed with the Almighty. He was always the most companionable and lovable of men—cheerful and jovial. Sometimes in our return home in the evening after we had been tramping around in the woods, he would call out: "Here, Mother, come David and Jonathan."

William continues:

> I said to him once: "Brother Joseph, don't you get frightened when all those hounding wolves are after you?"
>
> He answered: "No, I am not afraid; the Lord said he would protect me, and I have full confidence in his word."
>
> I knew the danger that whatever happened to him would happen to me, but I felt no more fear than I now feel. ... Life or death was a matter of indifference to me while I was the companion of the Lord's anointed.[18]

The second is the recollection of Jane Manning James, an African American woman about twenty years old, who was converted to the LDS Church in Connecticut about 1842. Anxious to join the Saints in Nauvoo, Jane wrote to Smith to say they were coming, and migrated with her mother, two sisters, a brother and sister-in-law and two small children—altogether eight persons. They walked

---

18. William Taylor, statement in "Recollections of Joseph Smith, the Prophet," *Young Woman's Journal* 16 (December 1905): 556.

all the way, approximately 1,000 miles. Jane had shipped by boat a trunk full of clothes she had been given which, however, was stolen at St. Louis, so the family arrived in Nauvoo in tattered rags; their shoes and stockings had long since worn out on the road. They were not a pretty sight when they arrived at Joseph and Emma Smith's home. Here is Jane's story:

> Sister Emma, she come to the door first, and she says, "Walk in, come in all of you." She went upstairs, and down [Joseph] comes and goes into the sitting room and told the girls [who were staying there], he wanted to have the room this evening, for we have got company come. ... He went and brought Dr. [John] Bernhisel down and introduced him to everyone of us, and said, "Now, I want you to tell me about some of your hard trials."...
>
> He kept our folks a whole week until they got homes, and I was left. He came in every morning to see us and shake hands and know how we all were. One morning before he came in, I had been up to the [steamboat] landing and found all my clothes were gone. Well, I sat there crying. He came in and looked around.
>
> "Why where's all the folks?"
>
> "Why brother," I says, "they have all got themselves places"; but, I says, "I haint got any place," and I burst out a-crying.
>
> "We won't have tears here," he says.
>
> "But I have got no home."
>
> "Well you've got a home here," he says. ... He went ... upstairs and brought Sister Emma down and says, "here's a girl who says she's got no home. Don't you think she's got a home here?" She says, "If she wants to stay here."
>
> And he says, "Do you want to stay here?"
>
> "Yes, sir," says I.
>
> We had come afoot, a thousand miles. We lay in bushes, and in barns and outdoors, and traveled until there was a frost just like a snow, and we had to walk on that frost. ... But I wanted to go to Brother Joseph.

I did not talk much to him, but every time he saw me he would say, "God bless you," and pat me on the shoulder. To Sister Emma, he said, "… go down to the store and clothe her up." Sister Emma did. She got me clothes by the bolt. I had everything. … He never passed me without shaking hands with me, wherever he was. Oh, he was the finest man I ever saw on earth.[19]

In June 1843, Smith became half-owner of the steamship *Maid of Iowa* and organized an excursion to Quincy, Illinois, for his family and friends, with a band on board to provide music. Among those in the party were Apostle Parley P. Pratt and his nine-year-old step-daughter, Mary Ann Stearns. After they had been fed and entertained by the mayor of Quincy, they returned to Nauvoo, a trip that took, because of the small steamer, most of the night. In the evening on the boat, friends gathered around Smith and he began to preach. Mary Ann recalled: "Because I was tired and sleepy, my Pa [Parley Pratt] took me on his lap to rest. He was sitting on the dock opposite Bro. Joseph, so near that their knees almost touched. … He [Joseph] stopped [for a minute] and gently raised my feet upon his knees, and when I would have drawn them away he said, "No. Let me hold them; you will rest better." I was soon sound asleep, and the next I knew, it was morning, and we had landed at Nauvoo."[20]

Another story of the Nauvoo period was from a woman for whom Smith did babysitting, of sorts. A native of Vermont, Philindia Eldredge was married to Levi Merrick at age eighteen and they settled in Apple Prairie, Illinois. Baptized by Parley Pratt in 1832, the Merricks moved to the Haun's Mill area, on Shoal Creek, Missouri, where they farmed. In the infamous Haun's Mill Massacre of October 30, 1838, Levi Merrick and their son Charles were both killed. As a

---

19. Jane James, statement in *Young Woman's Journal* 16 (December 1905): 551–53.

20. Mary Ann Stearns (Pratt) Winters, Reminiscences, LDS Church History Library; see also her statement in "Joseph Smith, The Prophet," *Young Woman's Journal* 16 (December 1905): 557–58.

young widow with three small children, Philindia moved to Nauvoo, where she supported herself by sewing and keeping house. She was one of the eighteen women who attended the first meeting of the Female Nauvoo Relief Society. Philindia did much of the sewing for the Joseph and Emma Smith family. Smith occasionally stayed with the Merrick children. "During those occasions he taught Philindia's little daughter Fannie to knit, and together they knitted a set of stockings for her little kitten."[21] In later life, Fannie related to her grandchildren many stories told her while she sat upon Smith's lap.

The next account is told by John R. Young, son of Brigham's younger brother Lorenzo and Persis Goodall Young. Born in Kirtland, Ohio, in 1837, John crossed the plains to the Salt Lake Valley in 1847 ("I was everybody's chore boy"). On his return home from the Sandwich Islands (Hawaii), because of the Utah War during the winter of 1857–58, he stopped in California to visit John M. Horner. A member of the church and one of California's leading agriculturists, Horner had been a boyhood friend of John Young in Nauvoo. Here is John Young's report of their visit:

> Mr. Horner told me that when he was a boy, Joseph [Smith] the Prophet and Oliver Cowdery had called on the Horner family. John M. wanted to visit with the young Prophet; but his father insisted that he finish hoeing a piece of corn given him as a stint [i.e., chore]. Joseph, on learning took off his coat, asked for a hoe, and helped finish the task. The sequel: John Horner was baptized by Oliver Cowdery, and confirmed and blessed by Joseph Smith, who predicted that the earth should yield abundantly at Brother Horner's behest. In California, Brother Horner [a truck gardener during the Gold Rush] at one time paid a tithe of twenty thousand dollars, the fruit of agriculture.[22]

---

21. See "Philindia Eldredge Merrick," in Kate Carter, ed., *Heart Throbs of the West*, 12 vols. (Salt Lake City: Daughters of Utah Pioneers, 1936–48), 4:240–41.

22. *Memoirs of John R. Young, Utah Pioneer, 1847* (Salt Lake City: Privately published, 1920), 142.

John R. Young, of course, also knew Smith:

> One day father took me for a walk, to give me air and sunshine. [John was four years old.] We met Joseph and Hyrum Smith and Sidney Rigdon. Father shook hands warmly with Joseph and Hyrum, but he merely bowed to Brother Rigdon. Joseph asked if I was the child father had requested the elders to pray for. Being answered in the affirmative, the prophet removed my hat, ran his fingers through my curly locks, and said, "Brother Lorenzo, this boy will live to aid in carrying the Gospel to the nations of the earth." His words thrilled me like fire; and from that hour I looked forward to the day I should be a missionary.[23]

John Young served missions to southern Utah in 1861, again to Hawaii in 1864, and to England in 1877, and left a splendid book of *Memoirs*.

Helen Mar Kimball Whitney, the daughter of Heber C. Kimball, who kept some of her father's diary and wrote much early church history, commented: "Joseph [Smith] was noted for his child-like love and familiarity with children, and he never seemed to feel that he was losing any of his honor or dignity in doing so. And if he heard the cry of a child, he would rush out of the house to see if it was harmed."[24] George Q. Cannon also wrote of Smith's "deep feeling for both children and animals," and in his *Life of Joseph Smith* gave stories to illustrate.[25]

Here is the kind of recreation the Saints enjoyed under Smith's direction in Nauvoo. On February 20, 1843, a "woodcutting bee" was held at the Smiths' home. Seventy brethren attended. They sawed,

---

23. Ibid., 10.

24. Helen Mar Whitney, "Scenes in Nauvoo," *Woman's Exponent* 11 (March 1, 1883): 146.

25. George Q. Cannon, *The Life of Joseph Smith, The Prophet* (Salt Lake City: Juvenile Instructor Office, 1888), 204. See also a talk by Jesse N. Smith to a church history class at LDS College in Salt Lake City in 1905, printed in *Journal of Jesse Nathaniel Smith*, 454–55.

chopped, split, and piled up a large stack of wood in the yard, which served not only Smith's family, but also the many persons whom they assisted. "The day was spent by them with much pleasantry, good humor, and feeling," reports the record. "A white oak log measuring five feet four inches in diameter, was cut through with a cross-cut saw, in four-and-a-half minutes, by Hyrum Dayton and Brother John Tidwell." This tree had been previously cut by Joseph himself, and he had hauled it to the yard with his team.[26]

Another example of such recreation is told by Mosiah Hancock:

> That summer [1841], I played my first game of ball with the Prophet [Joseph Smith]. We took turns knocking and chasing the ball, and when the game was over the Prophet said, "Brethren, hitch up your teams"; which we did, and we all drove to the woods. I drove our one-horse wagon standing on the front bolster, and Brother Joseph and father rode ... behind. There were 39 teams in the group and we gathered wood until our wagons were loaded. When our wagon was loaded, Brother Joseph offered to pull sticks with anyone—and he pulled them all up one at a time—with anyone who wanted to compete with him. Afterwards the Prophet sent the wagons out to different places of people who needed help; and he told them to cut the wood for the Saints who needed it. Everybody loved to do as the Prophet said.[27]

Later, the first governor of the state of California, Peter Burnett, a lawyer in Missouri in the 1830s, was sometimes engaged to represent Latter-day Saint leaders in court cases. After relating several experiences with Smith, intended to show that he was a man of courage, resourcefulness, and high intelligence, Burnett wrote:

> [Joseph Smith] was much more than an ordinary man. He possessed

---

26. See E. Cecil McGavin, *Nauvoo the Beautiful* (Salt Lake City: Stevens & Wallis, 1946), 59.

27. Autobiography of Mosiah Hancock, 22, L. Tom Perry Special Collections, Harold B. Lee Library, Brigham Young University, Provo, Utah.

the most indomitable perseverance, was a good judge of men, and deemed himself born to command, and he did command. His views were so strange and striking, and his manner so earnest, and apparently so candid, that you could not but be interested. There was a kind, familiar look about him that pleased you. He was very courteous in discussion, readily admitting what he did not intend to controvert, and would not oppose you abruptly, but had due deference to your feelings. He had the capacity for discussing a subject in different aspects, and for proposing many original views, even of ordinary matters. His illustrations were his own. He had great influence over others.[28]

A boy of nine accompanied his father, Byram Bybee, with his team and wagon to the quarry to get stone for the Nauvoo temple in the early 1840s. When they started, their wagon became stuck in a mud hole. As the father stepped off the wagon to get help, he encountered Smith who was walking to the temple. T. Edgar Lyon told the following story as related to him by the son:

> The man waded into the mud and said to the father, "Brother Bybee, you get by that left rear wheel and put your right shoulder under a spoke. I'll get my left shoulder under a spoke of the right wheel." Then to the … boy he said: "Get your whip ready and when I say 'Lift' we'll lift with our shoulders, and don't you spare the horseflesh."
>
> So saying, each in position, the man said "Lift." Each did his part. The horses jumped at the sting of the whip, the wagon moved a bit, and the horses were able to keep it going. After going about a hundred feet onto dry ground the boy let the team rest. The two men caught up with the wagon and as Brother Bybee climbed up to the driver's seat and took the reins from his son, the father called out, "Thank you, Brother Joseph."
>
> The boy had been greatly impressed that a prophet of the Lord,

---

28. Peter H. Burnett, *An Old California Pioneer* (Oakland, California: Biobooks, 1946), 39–40.

probably on his way to pay his temple tithing in labor, was not above wading in mud halfway to his knees and getting his shoulder covered with mud to help another man in distress.[29]

A final story reveals Smith's capacity for quiet heroism. He drove one evening with John Lyman Smith, his nine-year-old cousin, to a friend's house for supper. As they were finishing their meal, they heard a disturbance outside. A mob had gathered and was angrily yelling threats of murder, demanding that the host surrender Joseph Smith and his young cousin. Instead, the host led the Smiths through a back door and helped them escape in the darkness.

When the mob discovered that their quarry had fled, riders were dispatched along the main road they expected the Smiths would take. John Smith relates the rest of the story:

> Joseph and I did not take to the main road, however, but walked through the woods and swamps away from the road. We were helped by the bonfires [lit by our pursuers]. Pretty soon I began to falter in our flight. Sickness and fright had robbed me of strength. Joseph had to decide whether to leave me to be captured by the mob or to endanger himself by rendering aid. Choosing the latter course, he lifted me upon his own broad shoulders and bore me with occasional rests through the swamp and darkness. Several hours later we emerged upon the lonely road and soon reached safety. Joseph's herculean strength permitted him to accomplish this task and saved my life.[30]

These and other examples that might be mentioned demonstrate that Smith was many things to many people. A very human being, he did things that appealed to children, young people, and old people.

---

29. Lyon, "Recollections of 'Old Nauvooers,'" 147–48.

30. See Leonard J. Arrington, "Joseph Smith," in Arrington, *The Presidents of the Church* (Salt Lake City: Deseret Book Co., 1986), 31; "Newel Knight's Journal," in *Scraps of Biography* (Salt Lake City: Juvenile Instructor Office, 1883), 63–65; *Young Woman's Journal* 2 (November 1890): 76–77.

He enjoyed games, dinners, and prayer circles. He helped people with their problems and he shared their tragedies and triumphs. It is significant that people usually referred to him as "Brother Joseph," not as "President Smith." He was also a spiritual leader—orator, organizer, teacher, revelator—who was conversant about divine things. With a mind that was alive and alert, faith and intellect were partners in achieving both spiritual and temporal goals. The works he published, whatever his own contribution to their substance and wording, were sophisticated, had significant, intellectual content, and are worthy of the attention of students of American intellectual history.[31] Smith exercised leadership in relating individual members and the group to the universe and to society at large, he legitimated church authority and defined its responsibilities, and he interpreted the church's historical role.

Those who worked with Smith knew that he had strengths and weaknesses, but they believed in his divine calling. Their love of him and their faith in his calling shaped their lives. Smith said of himself, "I do not, nor never have pretended to be any other than a man, subject to passion and liable without the assisting grace of the Savior, to deviate from that perfect path in which all are commanded to walk."[32] He also said, "God is my friend, in him I shall find comfort. I have given my life unto His hands. I am prepared to go at his call and desire to be with Christ. I count not my life dear to me only to do his will."[33]

As LDS historian Marvin Hill has written, "Those who would understand the Prophet [Joseph Smith] must give consideration to his spiritual side as well as his human side. It was his strong

---

31. See Thomas O'Dea, *The Mormons* (Chicago: University of Chicago Press, 1967), 22–40.

32. *Latter-day Saints' Messenger and Advocate* 1 (December 1834): 40.

33. Joseph Smith, Letter to Emma Smith, June 6, 1832, Joseph Smith Letters, Archives-Library, Community of Christ, Independence, Missouri.

commitment to things spiritual which made him so aware of his human failings, so desirous to overcome his weaknesses and to give his all to the work of the Lord."[34]

o o o

Smith did not work alone. With respect to other early LDS leaders, Sidney Rigdon, a counselor to Smith from 1832 to 1844, contributed most of the "Lectures on Faith" that were an early attempt to present a systematic theology. A student of the scriptures, Rigdon also delivered many sermons that related to such principles and ordinances as faith, repentance, baptism, spiritual gifts, the Millennium, and communitarianism. Rigdon played an important role in 1832 when he and Smith, "in the midst of a magnificent glory," recorded a revelation now known as Section 76 of the Doctrine and Covenants. This revelation contains the LDS doctrines of the mission of Jesus Christ; the nature of Satan; the so-called sons of perdition; the celestial, terrestrial, and telestial degrees of resurrected glory; and the eternal destiny of the human family on the earth.[35]

A second influence on early LDS thought was that made by Parley P. Pratt and his brother Orson Pratt. Parley Pratt wrote *Voice of Warning* (1837), *Key to the Science of Theology* (1855), *The Autobiography of Parley Parker Pratt* (1874), and founded the *Latter-day Saints' Millennial Star* (Liverpool, 1840–1970). Parley's younger

---

34. Marvin S. Hill, "Joseph Smith the Man: Some Reflections on a Subject of Controversy," *BYU Studies* 21 (Spring 1981): 186.

35. For Rigdon's biography, see Richard S. Van Wagoner, *Sidney Rigdon: A Portrait of Religious Excess* (Salt Lake City: Signature Books, 1994); see also F. Mark McKiernan, *"The Voice of One Crying in the Wilderness": Sidney Rigdon, Religious Reformer, 1793–1876* (Lawrence, Kansas: Coronado Press, 1971); Joseph W. White, "The Influence of Sidney Rigdon Upon the Theology of Mormonism," (master's thesis, University of Southern California, 1947); and Daryl Chase, "Sidney Rigdon: Early Mormon," (master's thesis, University of Chicago, 1931). On the "Lectures on Faith," see Larry E. Dahl and Charles D. Tate, eds., *The Lectures on Faith in Historical Perspective* (Provo, Utah: BYU Religious Studies Center, 1990).

Sidney Rigdon *Parley P. Pratt*

brother, Orson, sometimes regarded as the foremost LDS intellectual of the nineteenth century, wrote a series of pamphlets for distribution in England, which gave philosophical meaning and depth to many of the theological teachings. Many of these were important enough to be reviewed in some important literary and philosophical journals in Europe.[36]

Emma Hale Smith wrote letters for her prophet-husband, penned revelations and blessings, discussed doctrines and practices, pointed out errors and shortcomings, and handled church business

36. See Teryl L. Givens and Matthew J. Grow, *Parley P. Pratt: The Apostle Paul of Mormonism* (New York: Oxford University Press, 2011); Reva Stanley, *A Biography of Parley P. Pratt: The Archer of Paradise* (Caldwell, Idaho: Caxton Printers, 1937); Parley P. Pratt, ed., *The Autobiography of Parley Parker Pratt* (New York: Russell Brothers, 1874); Breck England, *The Life and Thought of Orson Pratt* (Salt Lake City: University of Utah Press, 1985); T. Edgar Lyon, "Orson Pratt—Early Mormon Leader," (master's thesis, University of Chicago, 1932); Joseph W. Tingey, "An Explication of Some Philosophical Aspects of the Thought of Orson Pratt," (master's thesis, Brigham Young University, 1958); and N. B. Lundwall, comp., *Masterful Discourses of Orson Pratt* (Salt Lake City: N. B. Lundwall, n.d.). See also Gary James Bergera, *Conflict in the Quorum: Orson Pratt, Brigham Young, Joseph Smith* (Salt Lake City: Signature Books, 2002). A book that places Orson Pratt in the context of Mormon theological speculation and the findings and speculations of nineteenth-century science is Erich Robert Paul, *Science, Religion, and Mormon Cosmology* (Urbana: University of Illinois Press, 1992).

Orson Pratt

Emma Hale Smith

in Smith's absence.[37] In August 1842, when remembering a visit with Emma, Smith paid her a special tribute: "With what unspeakable delight, and what transports of joy swelled my bosom, when I took by the hand my beloved Emma—she that was my wife ... and the choice of my heart. Many were the reverberations of my mind when I contemplated for a moment the many scenes we had been called to pass through, the fatigues and the toils, the sorrows and sufferings, and the joys and consolations, [for] she is undaunted, firm, and unwavering—unchangeable, affectionate Emma!"[38]

In addition to giving birth to nine children and serving as mother to two adopted children, Emma Smith also was active in defense of her husband's legal rights, served as president of the Female Relief Society, and compiled the church's first hymnal.

The cultivation of faith and intellect that Smith and his associates preached meant that the Latter-day Saints as individuals and as families would laugh together just as they prayed together; that they would recognize the weaknesses as well as the great strengths

---

37. See Linda King Newell and Valeen Tippetts Avery, *Mormon Enigma: Emma Hale Smith* (Garden City, New York: Doubleday, 1984).

38. Qtd. in B. H. Roberts, ed., *History of the Church ...*, 6 vols., 2nd ed. (Salt Lake City: Church of Jesus Christ of Latter-day Saints, 1946ff.), 5:107.

of their humanity; that they would become warm and engaging persons; and that they would take pleasure in remaining faithful to the gospel.

Let me conclude with a bit of semi-comical poetry apparently composed on the spur of the moment by Smith. Barbara Matilda Neff, the daughter of a well-to-do eastern family, visited Nauvoo as a newly baptized member of the church in 1842 and began an autograph book, as did many other teenage girls.[39] This book, with the messages and signatures of the first eight presidents of the LDS Church and many other prominent leaders, both men and women, begins with an autograph by W. W. Phelps, who wrote two favorite LDS hymns, "Now Let Us Rejoice" and "The Spirit of God." In Neff's autograph book, Phelps wrote this brief rhymed message:

Two things will beautify a youth
That is: Let virtue decorate the truth.
And so you know; every little helps
    Yours, W. W. Phelps

Smith was asked to sign on the second page. He responded in the same vein:

The truth and virtue both are good
When rightly understood
But charity is better Miss
That takes us home to bliss
And so forthwith
    Remember Joseph Smith

---

39. Neff's autograph book is in the LDS Church History Library.

CHAPTER 2

Brigham Young

PRACTICAL LEADER AND VISIONARY

Just as Joseph Smith had been the dominant figure in the early LDS Church, Brigham Young (1801–77) was the most prominent person in pioneer Mormon Country. He was the first governor of Utah territory, the first superintendent of Indian Affairs, the founder of many industries and enterprises, the leading colonizer, and president of the church from 1847 until his death thirty years later. As Smith had been with early members, Young came close to being all things to all Latter-day Saints. He supervised the construction of houses, canals, roads, and the erection of fences. He counseled settlers on farm operations; household management, relationships with wives, husbands, and children; and on the husbanding of cash. A talented organizer, Young formed LDS wards and stakes, established courts and community offices, helped to obtain machinery and equipment for the erection and operation of mills and factories, and fostered cordial relations with Native Americans in the region.[1]

Living on the frontier of western New York as a child and young

---

1. Biographies of Young include Leonard J. Arrington, *Brigham Young: American Moses* (New York: Alfred A. Knopf, 1985): Eugene England, *Brother Brigham* (Salt Lake City: Bookcraft, 1980); Francis M. Gibbons, *Brigham Young: Modern Moses, Prophet of God* (Salt Lake City: Deseret Book Co., 1981); M. R. Werner, *Brigham Young* (New York: Harcourt, Brace, and Co., 1925); and Susa Young Gates, in collaboration with Leah D. Widtsoe, *The Life Story of Brigham Young* (New York: Macmillan, 1930). See also John G. Turner, *Brigham Young: Pioneer Prophet* (Cambridge, Massachusetts: Harvard University Press, 2012).

man, Young had only eleven days of formal schooling. His mother, who suffered from tuberculosis, helped Young, who sometimes carried her from bed to table and back to bed, by schooling him in reading, writing, and arithmetic. He read the Bible daily, kept informed of current events by reading the newspaper, and listened to visiting preachers and other educated persons. As the ninth child in a family of eleven, he learned to cook, keep house, clear fields of timber and brush, plant and tend crops, trap animals and birds, and occasionally attended religious meetings. He was bright, inquisitive, and interested in almost everything.

Young's mother died when he was fifteen, his father remarried, and Young went out into the world to make a living. He apprenticed to a carpenter, a painter, and then a cabinetmaker. He took contracts to build, paint, and do interior woodwork. By his early twenties, he was regarded as a skilled craftsmen in western New York. Some of the homes he built and furniture he made still exist, still admired, and furnish examples of early American handwork. When he was twenty-three, he married Miriam Angeline Works (b. 1806), and they became the parents of two girls. His wife, however, contracted tuberculosis (then the principal killer in America) and died in 1832.

Young had seen a copy of the Book of Mormon when it was first published in 1830, and he became convinced of its authenticity. But he postponed baptism until he had determined that the members and officers of the church manifested "right good sense." In 1832, after the death of his wife, he joined his older brother Phinehas Young (1799–1879) and his neighbor and friend Heber C. Kimball in journeying to Kirtland, Ohio, to see Joseph Smith. Here is Young's report of that meeting:

> We went to his father's house and learned that he [Joseph Smith] was chopping wood. We immediately went to the woods, where we found the Prophet and two or three of his brothers.

Here my joy was full at the privilege of shaking the hand of the Prophet of God, and I received the sure testimony, by the spirit of prophecy, that he was all that any man could believe him to be, as a true prophet. He was happy to see us, and made us welcome.

In the evening a few of the brethren came in, and we conversed together upon the things of the kingdom. Joseph called upon me to pray. In my prayer I spoke in tongues, which gift I had previously received and exercised. As soon as we arose from our knees, the brethren flocked around him [Joseph] and asked his opinion concerning the gift of tongues that was upon me. He told them that it was the pure Adamic language. Some said to him they expected he would condemn the gift Brother Brigham had, but he said, "No, it is of God, and the time will come when Brother Brigham Young will preside over this Church."[2]

Somewhat later, Young declared, "I feel like shouting hallelujah all the time, when I think that I ever knew Joseph Smith, the Prophet whom the Lord raised up and ordained, and to whom He gave the keys and power to build up the Kingdom at God on earth and sustain it."[3]

From the time of that first meeting, Young strove to learn all he could from Smith. He was with him on Zion's Camp; he directed the Saints' migration from Missouri to Illinois when Smith was in Liberty Jail; and he served as one of Smith's trusted advisors. Young boasted, "I do not think that a man lives on the earth that knew him any better than I did; and I am bold to say that, Jesus Christ excepted, no better man ever lived or does live upon this earth."[4]

Young became an apostle in 1835, led a group of apostles in a missionary effort in Great Britain in 1839–41, served as a business manager of the church until Smith's death in 1844, and from his

---

2. *Latter-day Saints' Millennial Star* 25 (July 11, 1863): 439.

3. Sermon of October 6, 1855, *Journal of Discourses,* 26 vols. (Liverpool, England: Latter-day Saints Booksellers Depot, 1854–86), 3:51 (hereafter JD).

4. Sermon of August 3, 1862, JD 9:332.

Brigham Young

position as president and senior member of the Quorum of Twelve Apostles succeeded Smith as leader of the Latter-day Saints in 1844. He was formally sustained as president of the church in 1847, the year he led the advance company of pioneers to the Salt Lake Valley.

As Smith had been, Young was also a persuasive speaker.[5] He believed that most Christian sermons were too formal and other-worldly. Instead, he spoke earnestly about everyday and practical concerns. In a spirited manner, he castigated the malfeasant politicians in Washington, DC, warned his people to expect more of the same kind of treatment unless they repented and united, and pled with them to obey their leaders. Let the idle find employment, he said—the discouraged seek to obtain the Spirit of God. He often closed with a ringing affirmation of his testimony of Smith and the eventual victory of the Mormon Restoration. Between such items,

---

5. On Young's impression of Smith as a "plain speaker," see his sermon of October 14, 1860, JD 8:206.

he delivered nuggets of doctrinal wisdom. He sometimes used stern images and folksy humor, and conducted impatient chastenings, but his primary focus was to maintain the unity of the Latter-day Saints in the face of political, legal, social, and military pressure.[6]

Regarding Young as an arresting speaker, Richard Burton, the celebrated English explorer, recalled the scene in 1860: "... *that* old man held his cough; *that* old lady awoke with a start; *that* child ceased the squall. Mr. Brigham Young ... [leaned] slightly forwards upon both hands propped on the green baize of the tribune [and] addressed his followers."[7]

Young was no more a formal theologian than Smith. He considered himself a practical man whose religion was centered in earthly concerns and pragmatic admonitions. When his more educated colleagues voiced their speculative instincts, he curbed and corrected their effulgences in the light of New England common sense. He believed in a simple gospel. Once, in 1857, after listening to one of Apostle Orson Pratt's long, involved arguments, he declared, "[It] makes me think, 'O dear, granny, what a long tail our puss has got!'"[8] Young's scattered, unsystematized theological pronouncements were generally directed to the here-and-now. His great overriding vision was the literal establishment of the Kingdom of God in the valleys of the mountains. The Mormon village was a covenant community, based on the concept of gathering for those who had been converted in the East and foreign lands.

There was in Young's theology something of the medieval ideal

---

6. On Young's thought, see John A. Widtsoe, ed., *Discourses of Brigham Young* (Salt Lake City: Deseret Book Co., 1941); Carl J. Furr, "The Religious Philosophy of Brigham Young," (PhD diss., University of Chicago, 1937); and H. Carleton Marlow, "Brigham Young's Philosophy of History," (master's thesis, Brigham Young University, 1959).

7. Richard F. Burton, *City of the Saints* ... (New York: Harper & Brothers, Publishers, 1862), 261.

8. Sermon of March 8, 1857, JD 4:267.

of community. For him, the injunction, "The earth is the Lord's and the fullness thereof," was not simply a poetical metaphor. God ruled. Young and his fellow Saints were human stewards erecting at long last the divine commonwealth. Its citizens must yield personal desires to the whole. Temporal and spiritual unity and equality were emphasized. Every activity of daily life was part of religion: "We cannot talk about spiritual things without connecting with them temporal things, neither can we talk about temporal things without connecting spiritual things with them. ... We, as Latter-day Saints, really expect, look for and we will not be satisfied with anything short of being governed and controlled by the word of the Lord in all of our acts, both spiritual and temporal. If we do not live for this, we do not live to be one with Christ."[9]

Young's corporate view suggested both godly omnipotence and an ordered universe. The Providential Hand arranged and molded events, chastised and rewarded participants, and worked to conclude a predetermined design. Young saw laws as eternal; the law of personal freedom, the law of rewards and punishments, the law of growth and decay, the law of procreation, and the law of organization.

Although Young realized that environment and events limited human agency, still enough individual freedom remained to allow humankind to choose good or evil. Correct choices, in turn, were rewarded by unending personal growth and the opportunity for eternal procreation. His eschatology for the righteous climaxed with the promise of a harmonious social order based upon enduring family relationships. Conversely, evil acts would bring upon the offenders diminution of self, the loss of increase, and inferior social organization.[10]

While he frequently urged, cajoled, and reproved his congregations, Young never preached depravity or damnation. He believed

---

9. Sermon of June 24, 1864, JD 10:329.

10. In addition to the sources mentioned above, see Arrington, *Brigham Young*, chapters 12 and 17.

that men and women were good, perfectible, and possessed of the divine. To realize their potential, they must be liberated from erroneous tradition. They were, in fact, gods in embryo, men and women seeking a heavenly partnership. Such a lofty, optimistic opinion of humankind, when joined with his view that men should never seek gifts from God that sweat and sinew could independently achieve, proved enormously energizing. It was a theology of empire building.

At every turn, Young pulled his theology and metaphysics earthward. Having an understanding of human nature, he believed that self-discovery brought a knowledge of God, and he accordingly molded his theology around daily human experience. Thus, his laws of freedom, reward, growth, procreation, and organization were earthly as well as heavenly. They could be validated by experience. When asked why God's hand did not more often intercede for the Saints, Young replied, "Man is destined to be a God, has to act as an independent being, and is left [by God] to see what he will do, to practice depending on his own resources, to be righteous in the dark, to do the best he can when left to himself to show his capacity."[11] The mission and responsibility of men and women, their destiny and privilege, Young said, was to build society—to plant trees, gardens, and vineyards; to build houses, shops, and meetinghouses; to dig ditches and dugways; to organize schools, concerts, and study classes. The whole face of the earth must be beautiful until it shall become like the Garden of Eden.[12] A prime imperative is to keep learning—to grow, to develop, and to have joy.

Empiricism undergirded all this thought; Young was eminently practical. Both Smith and he believed that if the realm of God was

---

11. Brigham Young, Office Journal, January 28, 1857, 6, in Brigham Young Office Files, 1832–1878, Church History Library, Church of Jesus Christ of Latter-day Saints, Salt Lake City, Utah, hereafter LDS Church History Library.

12. Sermon of June 5, 1853, JD 1:254.

to have any applicability to humankind, it must be explicable in terms men and women could understand and employ in their daily lives. If, on the other hand, the heavens operated on principles fundamentally different from the earth, he could see little hope or relevancy in discussing them. Young believed that revelations came frequently and that they were based on natural principles—not always (perhaps seldom) conveyed by ineffable experiences. Yet he did have an interior life of rich spirituality. He prayed—in private, in his family circle, and in council meetings and congregations. And he was a devoted participant in sacred ceremonies. There Young, removed from the ordinary routine of life, experienced an approach to God. He was responsive to the chords of celestial music as mediated through the liturgical experiences of the Salt Lake Endowment House and the Nauvoo and, later, St. George temples. In most respects, Young's theology was simple, literalistic, and conservative in the LDS context.

Young's innermost thoughts and desires are revealed by the vision he had for the kingdom—a vision partially revealed by the actual form that Mormon society took under his guiding hand. His vision derived partly from the idealized "City of Zion" conceived by Smith, but just as importantly from Young's own New York–New England sense of harmony and beauty, thrift and industry. From those two images, Young fused his ideal of a cooperatively organized familial or patriarchal society carving out a kingdom of peace in the midst of a world headed for disaster. The gospel had been restored, the priesthood authority was again on the earth, the keys of the kingdom were with the leaders of the church. God's purposes were being unfolded, and the Saints were part of it all. Indeed, the Saints were partners with God in transforming the desert wilderness into a productive homeland. In their isolation, they created a self-conscious and distinctive subculture, something equivalent to an ethnic society. Life on the frontier was hard, but it was a shared struggle and there was a cooperative spirit that continued after Young's death.

An important challenge to Young's leadership came in 1869 when a group of British Saints, who had converted to the LDS Church and "gathered" to Utah in the 1850s, began to publish editorials critical of Young's policies of economic containment in their *Utah Magazine*. With the approach of the transcontinental railroad in 1868, Young, fearing that the end of isolation would lead to political and economical involvement with "Babylon," inaugurated a "Protective Movement." The church would prevent or minimize an influx of those who might threaten the morality of Zion; establish locally owned cooperative enterprises to make the LDS community less dependent on imports from "outside"; canalize imports through a church-established wholesale concern, Zion's Cooperative Mercantile Institution (ZCMI); build interior branch railroads to provide transportation within the territory; and cut down on personal consumption to raise money for the Perpetual Emigration Company which would bring to Zion "our brothers and sisters" who were in Europe.[13]

As a part of the "protective" program, Latter-day Saints were not to participate in or give encouragement to the expansion of mining for precious metals. What people needed to be prosperous, Young said, was "iron and coal, good hard work, plenty to eat, good schools, and good doctrine."[14] Mining of precious metals was too chancy—"the blanks in the lottery are numerous, while the prizes are few."[15] Since almost all the mines were owned by non-Mor-

---

13. See Leonard J. Arrington, *Great Basin Kingdom: An Economic History of the Latter-day Saints* (Cambridge, Massachusetts: Harvard University Press, 1958), 235–56.

14. Qtd. in Journal History of the Church, May 29, 1870, LDS Church History Library.

15. George A. Smith, *The Rise, Progress and Travels of the Church,* 2nd ed. (Salt Lake City, 1872), 60.

mons, Young and his associates worked against the conversion of their promised valley into a rip-roaring mining camp.

But William S. Godbe, Edward W. Tullidge, E. L. T. Harrison, W. H. Shearman, T. B. H. Stenhouse, and Henry W. Lawrence, all talented "liberals," campaigned for cooperation with the gentiles (non-Mormons), elimination of economic and social insularity, and the development of mining. The "Godbeites," as they were called, contended that the ruling priesthood of the LDS Church had exceeded "the spirit and genius of the gospel," that there was "lack of commercial sense" in some of Young's policies, and that "God Almighty had never intended that the priesthood do all the thinking." Here was a demonstration of the tension between those who contended for freedom of individual belief about doctrine and policy and those, like Young, who insisted on unity and conformity. Because of what he believed were the continuing attempts of federal officials to undermine the LDS commonwealth and the efforts of non-LDS Utah politicos to subvert LDS control, Young wanted the Saints to show solidarity and union. He favored excommunication for those who cast doubt on church leadership, sowed discord, and fostered disunity. At the excommunication trial of some of the Godbeites, Young declared: "Where is our liberty? In truth. Where is our freedom? In truth. In the truth of God. In truth no matter where it is found. Where is our strength? In truth. Where is our power and our wisdom? In truth. It is truth that we want, it is truth that exalts us. It is truth that makes us free. It is truth that will bring us into the celestial kingdom."

The church and the Kingdom of God, Young said, must be the family of heaven. It is not the goal of the Saints to raise confusion: "What is the result when every man is for himself? Why the devil is for the whole of them. … The Priesthood will not do your thinking, but it will help you to think correctly. We work in harmony with our Savior; we cooperate with the Son for the salvation of ourselves and the human family. He wants His brethren to be co-workers with Him. ... If we ever build up Zion we will be one. ... I do not pretend to be infallible, but the priesthood that I have on me is infallible."[16] Young's policy continued to be devoted to the preservation of the tightly reigned independent theocratic commonwealth that he envisioned.

All truth—scientific and philosophical as well as doctrinal—was a part of Mormonism. "Mormonism," Young said, "embraces all truth that is revealed and that is unrevealed, whether religious, political, scientific, or philosophical."[17] Such a pronouncement encouraged his followers not only to develop morally, but also to grow in knowledge and intelligence. The arts and sciences came from God and were designed for the good of the Lord's children. Since God operated on the basis of natural principles, learning more about the geology, chemistry, and other aspects of the order of nature was expected: "Every art and science known and studied by the children of men is comprised within the gospel. Where did the knowledge come from which has enabled men [and women] to accomplish such great achievements in science and mechanism [engineering] within the last few years? We know that knowledge is from God."[18] This approach encouraged some young Mormons to seek higher education in colleges and universities where they could make the best of their abilities.

Young had a higher opinion than one might expect of women and their worth in the Lord's Kingdom and encouraged them to develop their potential. He said: "We think the sisters ought to have

16. A summary of the church excommunication trial from which these excerpts are taken is in Arrington, *Brigham Young*, 355–60. See also Devery S. Anderson, ed., *The Salt Lake School of the Prophets, 1867–1883* (Salt Lake City: Signature Books, 2018), appendix 2.

17. Sermon of January 12, 1862, JD 9:149.

18. John A. Widtsoe, ed., *Discourses of Brigham Young* (Salt Lake City: Deseret Book Co., 1976), 246.

the privilege to study various branches of knowledge that they may develop the powers with which they are endowed. Women are useful, not only to sweep houses, wash dishes, make beds, and raise babies, but they may also stand behind the counter, study law and physic [medicine], or become good bookkeepers, and all this to enlarge their sphere of usefulness for the benefit of society at large. In following these things they but answer the design of their creation."[19] Under Young's leadership, women in LDS communities exercised an important influence in agriculture, medicine, and health, economic and business development, literature, education, and politics.

Young may not have been an intellectual as we define the term today, but he provided the basis for the development of intellectuality among the young people. Indeed, there was a flowering of learning in Utah that followed the revitalization of the University of Deseret in 1869. Young was a disciplinarian on the trail west, a hard-headed businessman, a practical politician, and a visionary prophet; but he could also be a kind and helpful human being—tender, understanding, and compassionate, and with a lively sense of humor.

I believe Young was a great man *personally*.[20] This helps to explain why many people were so willing to follow him, so willing to respond to his calls. He did not put on airs, he could be a good listener, and he was often willing to get his own hands dirty to help out. He tried to go out of his way to talk with everyone as he visited a new ward or Utah settlement. He attended their dances and participated in all their activities. He expressed appreciation for services people rendered on behalf of the church. When he went into a home and saw persons who were suffering from an injury or painful illness, he sometimes wept. When he observed families without adequate food, he instructed the local bishop to see that they were supplied from the local church storehouse.

---

19. Sermon of July 18, 1869, JD 13:61.

20. See especially Leonard J. Arrington, "Brother Brigham: The Human Side," *This People* 11 (Spring 1990): 26–32.

He paid the tuition for many young people to attend the University of Deseret—not only for his own children and adopted orphans but also for many others whose parents could not afford the fees.

Despite his capacity for humor and satire, Young had a deeply spiritual nature and an appreciation of spiritual phenomena. On a few occasions, like the one mentioned earlier, he exercised the spiritual gift of speaking in tongues. He was benefited by miracles and assisted in healing others. He had dreams and visions that so impressed him that he left a record of them. One that he remembered most vividly was a vision of the Saints as a united and righteous family. Another of his revelations was printed as Section 136 of the LDS Doctrine and Covenants.

Nevertheless, Young was not a self-righteous person, nor overly proud of himself or his role. He said: "There are weaknesses in men [and women] that I am bound to forgive, [because] I am right there myself. I am liable to mistakes, I am liable to prejudice, and I am just as set in my feelings as any man that lives. But I am where I can see the light, and I try to keep in the light."[21] Only under certain circumstances was he dictatorial or rigid in his counsel. He was realistic in realizing that not everybody would take his advice. "[My people and I are] like the boys with their sleds," he said. "We go up hill very slowly, but [we] quickly rush down again. We are apt ... to be slow to learn righteousness, and quick to run in the ways of sin."[22]

Young was a pragmatist, but he was also an idealist. Smith had revealed the Law of Consecration and Stewardship in 1831, and Young had witnessed its application and had been imbued with the related rhetoric.[23] He believed, with the early Saints, that members

---

21. Brigham Young, Office Journal, April 30, 1860, LDS Church History Library.
22. Sermon of December 29, 1867, JD 12:124.
23. Leonard J. Arrington, Feramorz Y. Fox, and Dean L. May, *Building the City of God: Community and Cooperation among the Mormons* (Salt Lake City: Deseret Book Co., 1976), 40, et passim.

of the church constituted a community or church family. They must labor together, just as they worshipped together; they must share with each other; and they must work to build up the Kingdom of God, not as individuals but as a group; not by competition but by cooperation; not by individual aggrandizement but by community development; not by profit-seeking but by working without thought of self. For most of his thirty-year presidency, he pushed to organize cooperative stores and industries and more tightly contained community United Orders.

The "divine" Law of Consecration and stewardship that moved Young so strongly remained as a goal of LDS aspiration, a symbol of Christian perfection, a forecast of a better future, a remembrance of the "oneness in mind and heart" that God had prescribed for his people. Young resisted the idea that the individual self is the sole foundation of values and the final arbiter of truth.

o o o

Brigham Young's appreciation for intellect was manifested by his calling George Q. Cannon (1827–1901), a bright, young immigrant from Great Britain, to serve as a counselor in his First Presidency.[24] Cannon inaugurated *The Juvenile Instructor* in 1866 to instruct young LDS men and women and, through the George Q. Cannon & Sons Publishing Company, printed a "Faith-Promoting Series" of journals, biographies, and personal histories. Above all, he promoted education: "Latter-day Saints are ardent friends of learning, true seekers after knowledge. They recognize in a good

---

24. See Cannon, "Twenty Years Ago: A Trip to California," *Juvenile Instructor* 4 (January–June 1869): intermittently in 12 issues, 6–92; Beatrice Cannon Evans and Janath Russell Cannon, eds., *Cannon Family Historical Treasury* (Salt Lake City: George Q. Cannon Family Association, 1967), 85–140; Joseph J. Cannon, "George Q. Cannon," *Instructor,* January 1944 through November 1945, a serialized biography; Orson F. Whitney, "George Quayle Cannon," in *History of Utah,* 4 vols. (Salt Lake City, 1892–1901), 4:659–63; and especially Davis Bitton, *George Q. Cannon: A Biography* (Salt Lake City: Deseret Book Co., 1999).

education the best of fortunes, it broadens the mind, creates liberal and noble sentiments, and fits the possessor for a more successful struggle with the obstacles of life. ... The possession of knowledge is of itself the highest pleasure."[25]

With his publications aimed primarily at the youth, Cannon was an important bridge between the first generation of church leaders and the late nineteenth-century church membership. He served as an assistant president and then in the First Presidency from 1873 to 1901 as a counselor to four church presidents. He was intelligent, articulate, and well-read, and had a wide circle of friends, both LDS and non-LDS. Next to Orson Pratt, he was probably the LDS pioneer who was recognized most widely for his faith and intellect.

Cannon was born on January 11, 1827, in Liverpool, England, the oldest of seven children of a family living on the Isle of Man. In 1840, when he was thirteen, his family was converted to the LDS Church by his uncle, John Taylor, then an apostle, and in 1842 moved to Liverpool on their way to Nauvoo, Illinois. Cannon's mother died on the ocean voyage from Liverpool; his father died in Nauvoo. A young orphan, he was taken into the Taylor home where he worked with his uncle on the *Times and Seasons* and *Nauvoo Neighbor,* as both a writer and printer. He was adopted by John Taylor in 1846 in the Nauvoo temple and came west with the Taylor family in 1847, when he was twenty.

In the fall of 1849, Cannon and two or three dozen young men were called to California to mine gold for the benefit of the church and some of its aging but faithful early members. They worked for almost a year, but their mining was not particularly successful. In the fall of 1850, Cannon and nine others were called to preaching missions in the Sandwich Islands (Hawaii). Although five of the elders returned to Utah when they met with little success with

---

25. *Juvenile Instructor* 27 (April 1, 1892): 210.

the white settlers in the Islands, Cannon remained, gained a certain competency in the language, and worked with the natives. He seems to have acquired the language quickly. According to reports, the natives loved and revered him. Within four years, an estimated 4,000 native Hawaiians had joined the church and Cannon began helping to translate the Book of Mormon into Hawaiian. In 1854, he returned to Salt Lake City to marry Elizabeth Hoagland (1835–82). The two moved to San Francisco to publish the Hawaiian Book of Mormon and the church's *Western Standard* magazine.

When the US Army's Utah Expedition arrived in the spring of 1858 to quell dissent, the *Deseret News* printing press was moved to Fillmore, Utah, and Cannon was appointed managing editor. He held this position and that of editor until 1880, when Charles W. Penrose (1832–1925) became editor-in-chief. Later in 1858, Cannon was sent to preside over the church's Eastern States Mission with instructions to influence eastern editors who were pressured by hostile influences.

In 1860, Cannon returned to Utah and was ordained an apostle; he was only twenty-seven. Sent to England with Apostles Charles C. Rich (1809–83) and Amasa M. Lyman (1813–77) to preside over the church's European Mission, he edited and published the *Latter-day Saints' Millennial Star,* remaining four years with the exception of part of 1862 when he was reassigned to Washington, DC, to lobby for Utah statehood. Back in Salt Lake City from 1864 to 1867, he worked as private secretary and assistant president to Brigham Young. He was named general superintendent of the church's Sunday schools in 1867, and held this position until his death in 1901. He founded the semi-monthly (after 1880 a monthly) *Juvenile Instructor* for the Sunday Schools. Profusely illustrated with faith-promoting drawings and artwork, the magazine continued in expanded form as the organ of the Sunday School until 1970.

George Q. Cannon   *Eliza R. Snow*

Cannon was a careful, thoughtful observer, a constant reader, and a student of people and policies. He was a "natural" diplomat, ready conversationalist, and popular speaker. He served in the Utah legislature, was often sent to Washington, DC, to lobby for the LDS Church, undertook several short-term religious missions, and, as mentioned earlier, supervised the *Deseret News*. "More than any of the Mormon leaders," as Orson F. Whitney wrote, "he was prepared to meet men of the world."[26]

Cannon was Utah's elected delegate to Congress in 1872, and served nine years. With his affable and engaging manner, his knowledge of departments and functions of government, and his wide acquaintance with people, he was a human book of ready reference. He was an able speaker in the House, and had wide influence. He was known as "smooth-bore Cannon." As Young's secretary and confidante, he was one of the three executors of Young's estate after Young died in 1877. As delegate to Congress, Cannon welcomed two US presidents to Utah: Ulysses S. Grant in 1875 and Rutherford B. Hayes in 1880. As an active member of the First Presidency,

---

26. Whitney, *History of Utah,* 4:661.

he helped promote the electric industry, mining, beet sugar, salt, Saltair, railroads, and many other enterprises.

Cannon's writings include *My First Mission* (Salt Lake City: Juvenile Instructor Office, 1879); *The Life of Nephi* (Salt Lake City: Juvenile Instructor Office, 1883); *The Latter-day Prophet* (Salt Lake City: Juvenile Instructor Office, 1900); *Young People's History of the Mormons* (Salt Lake City: Juvenile Instructor Office, 1890); *The Life of Joseph Smith, The Prophet* (Salt Lake City: Juvenile Instructor Office, 1888); and *The First Book of the Faith Promoting Series,* 2nd ed. (Salt Lake City: Juvenile Instructor Office, 1882). There were about 300 recorded sermons or discourses, and thousands of editorials and magazine and newspaper articles. He died in 1901 in California at the age of seventy-four.

Though none of Cannon's books suggests that he experienced tension between his faith and intellect at any stage of his life, he was too bright not to have been aware of conflicting viewpoints. Orson F. Whitney, himself a distinguished LDS intellectual, wrote of Cannon, "Possessed of an unusual mentality, he absorbed knowledge as a sponge takes in water, and what his quick and wide apprehension encompassed, his marvelous memory ever after retained."[27]

Cannon was among the finest orators in the church's history; a fine writer; a bright intellect, eloquent and magnetic. In 1900, just before his death, he returned to the Sandwich Islands, where he was almost an idolized guest of honor at the jubilee celebration of the opening of the church's mission fifty years before. He was crowned with garlands and escorted around the islands by those he had known and baptized fifty years earlier. He was visited by Queen Lili'uokalani (1838–1917), and at her request he blessed and baptized her.

A second intellectual on whom Brigham Young depended was

---

27. Ibid., 659–63.

Eliza R. Snow (1804–87).[28] Born in Massachusetts and reared in Ohio, Snow, who had lived as a governess in the household of Joseph and Emma Smith, was baptized in 1835. She wrote: "As I was reflecting on the wonderful events transpiring around me, I felt an indescribable, tangible sensation ... commencing at my head and enveloping my person and passing off at my feet, producing inexpressible happiness. Immediately following, I saw a beautiful candle with an unusual long, bright blaze directly over my feet. I sought to know the interpretation, and received the following, 'The lamp of intelligence shall be lighted over your path.'"[29]

Snow was the first secretary of the women's Nauvoo Relief Society, for which she drew up the constitution. In 1842, also, she was sealed as a plural wife to Joseph Smith.

After Smith's death in 1844, Snow became a plural wife of Brigham Young. Their relationship appears to have been platonic,

---

28. Sources on the life of Eliza Roxcy Snow Smith include Augusta Joyce Crocheron, "Eliza R. Snow Smith," in *Representative Women of Deseret* (Salt Lake City, 1884), 1–9; Andrew Jenson, ""Snow, Eliza Roxey," in *Latter-day Saint Biographical Encyclopedia*, 4 vols. (Salt Lake City, 1901), 1:693–97; Maureen Ursenbach Beecher, "Eliza R. Snow's Nauvoo Journal," *BYU Studies* 15 (Summer 1975): 391–416; Beecher, "The Eliza Enigma: The Life and Legend of Eliza R. Snow," in *Sister Saints,* ed. Vicky Burgess-Olson (Provo, Utah: BYU Press, 1978), 1–19; Janet Peterson and LaRene Gaunt, "Eliza R. Snow," in *Elect Ladies* (Salt Lake City: Deseret Book Co., 1990), 23–40; Beecher, "Eliza R. Snow," in Claudia L. Bushman, ed., *Mormon Sisters: Women in Early Utah* (Cambridge, Massachusetts: Emmeline Press, 1976), 24–41; and Karen Lynn Davidson and Jill Mulvay Derr, *The Life and Faith of Eliza R. Snow* (Salt Lake City: Deseret Book Co., 2013). Many of Snow's writings have been compiled and published as a separate volume: see Bryant S. Hinckley, LeRoi Snow, and Arthur M. Richardson, comps., *Eliza R. Snow, An Immortal; Selected Writings of Eliza R. Snow* (Salt Lake City: Nicholas G. Morgan Sr., Foundation, 1957); *Life and Labors of Eliza R. Snow Smith* (Salt Lake City: Juvenile Instructor Office, 1880); and especially Jill Mulvay Derr and Karen Lynn Davidson, comps. and eds., *Eliza R. Snow: The Complete Poetry* (Provo, Utah: Brigham Young University, 2013). See also Leonard J. Arrington, "The Legacy of Latter-day Saint Women," *John Whitmer Historical Association Journal* 10 (1990): 3–17; Maureen Ursenbach Beecher, *Eliza and Her Sisters* (Salt Lake City: Aspen Books, 1991).

29. Hinckley et al., *Eliza R. Snow, An Immortal,* 6.

she serving as an advisor, he as a provider. She always referred to him with nineteenth-century formality as "President Young"; he called her "Sister Snow."

In Salt Lake City, Snow directed the woman's section of the Endowment House (forerunner to the Salt Lake temple) on Temple Square, and gave instruction on prayers and administrations to midwives who were appointed to care for women who were about to give birth. Snow and several female associates often administered to sick women and children, a practice that had the support of Smith, Young, and other contemporary church authorities.

In 1854, with the help of her brother Lorenzo, Snow organized the Polysophical Society, a group that met bi-weekly in Lorenzo's home or the Seventies Hall. Snow referred to the meetings as a "magnificent moral, intellectual and spiritual picnic." There were speeches, songs, readings, recitations, instrumental music on guitar, organ, piano, and bagpipe. In a time of general male domination, the women were there as equals, performing as well as listening with their husbands and brothers, and Snow contributed often—poetry, essays, and inspirational thoughts.[30]

During this period, the Saints began to sing with increasing regularity Snow's poem "Invocation"—a popular LDS hymn now called "O My Father"—in which she vocalized a doctrine she said was taught by Smith, that there is a Heavenly Mother as well as a Heavenly Father. She was also the respected author of such beloved LDS hymns as "How Great the Wisdom and the Love," "Truth Reflects Upon Our Senses," and "Behold the Great Redeemer Die."

A charismatic, highly visible person, Snow was instrumental

---

30. Eliza R. Snow Smith, *Biography and Family Record of Lorenzo Snow* (Salt Lake City, 1884), 252–53. See also Maureen Ursenbach, "Three Women and the Life of the Mind," *Utah Historical Quarterly* 43 (Winter 1975): 26–40. Eliza published her first book of poems in 1856 under the title *Poems, Religious, Historical and Political* (Liverpool, 1856). A second volume was published in 1877. Both were ambitious projects; the first was 270 pages, the second 284 pages.

in the formation of churchwide Relief Societies in the 1850s and 1860s. As the number of Relief Societies grew, particularly after 1867, Snow was set apart as president of the sisterhood of the entire church, in which position she served until her death in 1887. She became, in effect, a counselor to Brigham Young on matters pertaining to women, and was often introduced as "Presidentess," assisted by other Relief Society leaders. Snow also formed in each LDS ward and settlement Young Ladies' Mutual Improvement Associations for young women from ages twelve to twenty-five, and Primary Associations for boys and girls from three to twelve.

On January 13, 1870, Snow presided at a mass meeting in the Old Tabernacle in Salt Lake City (where the Assembly Hall now stands), where some 6,000 women came to protest the passage by the US Congress of the Cullom Bill, an anti-polygamy bill that removed authority from local courts and juries, deprived wives of immunity as witnesses against their husbands, and authorized the use of the US military to enforce these and other federal regulations. Snow's address was strong and eloquent, as were those of other LDS women leaders. The meeting was given national coverage, and from that time Mormon women were regarded less by national commentators as submissive and degraded. A month later, the women of Utah agitated for and were granted suffrage, the first women in the nation to exercise this privilege. Now, as Snow observed, "no woman in Zion need mourn because her sphere is too narrow."[31]

Snow exerted another influence when she encouraged Utah women to go east to study medicine. Under her direction and with the financial support of the Relief Societies, Utah quite possibly had, around the turn of the twentieth century, the largest colony of trained women doctors of any region in the nation.[32]

---

31. "An Address by Miss Eliza R. Snow ... August 14, 1872," *Latter-day Saints' Millennial Star* 36 (January 13, 1874): 21.

32. Maureen Ursenbach Beecher, "A Decade of Mormon Women—the 1870s," *New Era* 8 (April 1978): 35–36.

In 1876–77, Snow directed the preparation of a manuscript which, with the assistance of Edward W. Tullidge, was published under the title *The Women of Mormondom* (New York, 1877). This book, containing the personal histories and important talks of twenty-six LDS women and shorter sketches of fifty-six additional women, was remarkable for the 1870s when women were just emerging as a visible force in LDS society and culture. The final paragraphs testify to the influence of Joseph Smith:

> Paul, in the egotism of man's apostleship, commanded, "let the woman be silent in the church," ... and the Prophet Joseph corrected Paul, and made woman a voice in the church, and endowed her with an apostolic ministry. ... First, woman in her ever blessed office of motherhood; next, in her divine ministry. ... Woman shall leaven the earth with her own nature. She shall leaven it in her great office of maternity, and in her apostolic mission. ... This is the woman's age. Woman must, therefore, lay the cornerstone of the new civilization.[33]

The idea of the 552-page book was Snow's; she induced the women to write the personal histories that form the basis of the book, and she raised the funds for its publication. Snow thus initiated the one book sketching the history of Mormon women before the revitalization of the women's movement in the 1960s and 1970s.

In the summer of 1878, seventy-four-year-old Snow and a few associates traveled to about 200 LDS settlements in Utah and surrounding states and territories. They held, in most cases, two meetings a day with local women residents. This was Snow's way of keeping in touch with the Relief Societies and the Young Ladies and Primary organizations. The women bore testimonies, sang hymns, spoke in tongues, and exercised spiritual gifts. Snow blessed the sick, administered to those who requested it, and washed and anointed

---

33. Edward R. Tullidge, *The Women of Mormondom* (New York, 1877), 541–51.

women about to give birth. It was Snow who taught the proper forms of the pre-birthing ritual that continued until the 1930s.[34]

In the remaining years of her life, 1880–87, Snow continued to organize and supervise Relief Societies, Young Ladies' Mutuals, and Primaries in local wards and settlements; made a special effort to work on behalf of Native American women; published a hymnal (Salt Lake City, 1880); prepared a book of *Bible Questions and Answers for Children* (Salt Lake City, 1881); assisted in establishing the Deseret Hospital, of which she was president; published a *First and Second Speaker* or book of recitations for the children's Primary Association (Salt Lake City, 1882); and completed her *Biography and Family Record of Lorenzo Snow* (Salt Lake City, 1884).

While one seldom finds any intellectual issues addressed by Snow in her books and letters, her poems reflect in veiled ways the seeds of such confrontations and struggles over plural marriage, the rights of women, Brigham Young's penchant for giving advice to girls and women, and such doctrinal issues as the nature of the resurrection and the existence of the Heavenly Mother. Snow accepted authority, but she sometimes challenged policies and procedures and, particularly on issues relating to women, was not timid in exerting her own authority.

Snow was also an intellectual center around whom women clustered for mental stimulation. A born leader, an efficient organizer, her firmly established convictions of the principles of the LDS gospel, as Emmeline B. Wells wrote, "gave her the confidence and assurance to act independently in places, and at times, when other women would have faltered or hesitated to undertake such heroic efforts."[35]

Snow died in Salt Lake City on December 5, 1887, at the age of

---

34. Beecher, "Eliza Enigma," 38.

35. Beecher, "Three Women and the Life of the Mind," 35–40; and Emmeline B. Wells, "L.D.S. Women of the Past: Personal Impressions," *Woman's Exponent* 36 (February 1908): 49–50.

eighty-three. She is buried in Brigham Young's private cemetery one block east of the Lion House in downtown Salt Lake City.

Under the leadership of Brigham Young, the hierarchical structure of the church continued. The revelations of Joseph Smith were canonized, and the doctrine and organizational structure of the church was firmly fixed. An accelerated educational program resulted in the founding of Brigham Young Academy in Provo, now Brigham Young University; the Brigham Young College in Logan, which later yielded to Utah State University; the University of Deseret and Latter-day Saints College in Salt Lake City that later withdrew in favor of the University of Utah; and many academies and high schools in the various settlements.

The way was prepared for the faith and intellectual contributions of Emmeline B. Wells, Susa Young Gates, and Alice Merrill Horne.

CHAPTER 3

Emmeline B. Wells

POET-JOURNALIST AND FEMINIST

On April 18, 1842, at the sixth meeting of the Female Relief Society in the Lodge Room of Joseph Smith's Red Brick Store in Naúvoo, Illinois, Smith gave instructions to the 200 members of the church's Relief Society founded just a few weeks earlier. After discussing the exercise of spiritual gifts and priesthood authority, Smith said he was now delivering the keys to "this [the Relief] Society and to the church … [because], according to his prayers, God had appointed him elsewhere." He then stated: "[Sisters], I now turn the key to you in the name of God, and this Society shall rejoice, and knowledge and intelligence shall flow down from this time. This is the beginning of better days for this Society."[1]

We know from a study of Smith's life that this was not an off-hand remark.[2] His task was the Restoration, an aspect of which

---

1. Minutes, Nauvoo Female Relief Society, April 18, 1842, Church History Library, Church of Jesus Christ of Latter-day Saints, Salt Lake City, Utah; hereafter LDS Church History Library. See also Jill Mulvay Derr, Janath Russell Cannon, and Maureen Ursenbach Beecher, *Women of Covenant: The Story of Relief Society* (Salt Lake City: Deseret Book Co., 1992); as well as Jill Mulvay Derr, Carol Cornwall Madsen, Kate Holbrook, and Matthew J. Grow, eds., *The First Fifty Years of Relief Society: Key Documents in Latter-day Saint Women's History* (Salt Lake City: Church Historian's Press, 2016).

2. Smith's attitudes toward women are discussed in Carol Cornwall Madsen, "Mormon Women and the Temple: Toward a New Understanding," in Maureen Ursenbach Beecher and Lavina Fielding Anderson, eds., *Sisters in Spirit: Mormon Women in Historical and Cultural Perspective* (Urbana: University of Illinois Press,

was restoring to women the status they enjoyed or were promised in early Christian communities.[3] In contrast to surrounding societies (Roman and eastern Mediterranean), as recent historians now contend, there apparently was an approach to equality between the sexes. Pointing his society in this direction was a sincere conviction that Smith believed was inspired.[4] Under God's blessing, he believed these women—and indeed all women—were to have a better day. The women of the infant church—those who were present at this 1842 meeting and at other gatherings where Smith spoke—believed this to be a revelation on their behalf. Seeing a gradual improvement in the position of women, in the church and in civilized society, they were quick to attribute the change to divine influences for good.

1987), 80–110; Linda King Newell, "Gifts of the Spirit: Women's Share," in *Sisters in Spirit*, 111–50; Jill Mulvay Derr, "'Strength in Our Union': The Making of Mormon Sisterhood," in *Sisters in Spirit*, 153–207; Leonard J. Arrington and Davis Bitton, *The Mormon Experience: A History of the Latter-day Saints* (New York: Alfred A. Knopf, 1979), 220–42; Leonard J. Arrington, "Persons for All Seasons: Women in Mormon History," *BYU Studies* 20 (Fall 1979): 39–58; and Carol Cornwall Madsen, "Mormon Women and the Struggle for Definition: The Nineteenth Century Church," *Sunstone* 6 (November–December 1981): 7–11.

3. See Ben Witherington III, *Women in the Earliest Churches* (Cambridge, England: Cambridge University Press, 1988).

4. Lucy Mack Smith (1775–1856), Joseph Smith's mother and a formidable, yet kindly, woman, undoubtedly helped to shape her son's attitude toward women. She demonstrated courage and helped her children realize a better day. As a frequent speaker at Relief Society meetings, she reasserted her son's promise as a sacred goal for the women to work toward. See Lucy Mack Smith, *Biographical Sketches of Joseph Smith the Prophet and His Progenitors for Many Generations* (Liverpool, England, 1853); Lavina Fielding Anderson, ed., *Lucy's Book: A Critical Edition of Lucy Mack Smith's Family Memoir* (Salt Lake City: Signature Books, 2010); Richard L. Bushman, *Joseph Smith and the Beginnings of Mormonism* (Urbana: University of Illinois Press, 1984); Richard Lyman Bushman, *Joseph Smith: Rough Stone Rolling* (New York: Alfred A. Knopf, 2005); Edward W. Tullidge, *Life of Joseph the Prophet* (Plano, Illinois: Board of Publication of the Reorganized Church of Jesus Christ of Latter Day Saints, 1880); Mary Audentia Smith Anderson, *Ancestry and Posterity of Joseph Smith and Emma Hale* (Independence, Missouri: Herald House, 1929); and Leonard J. Arrington and Susan Arrington Madsen, "Lucy Mack Smith," *Mothers of the Prophets* (Salt Lake City: Deseret Book Co., 1987), 2–26.

As we saw with Eliza Snow, Latter-day Saint women did lead out in many areas.[5] Focusing LDS feminist thought both before and after Snow's death in 1887 was Emmeline B. Wells. Wells was a woman of intellect, talented writing and editorial skills, determination, and perseverance. Improvement in the status of women dominated her life and thought.

Emmeline Blanche Woodward was born in Petersham, Worcester County, Massachusetts, on February 29, 1828, the seventh of nine children of descendants of early Puritan settlers.[6] Her grandfather fought in the Revolutionary War and her father, who died

5. See, especially, Claudia L. Bushman, ed., *Mormon Sisters: Women in Early Utah* (Cambridge, Massachusetts: Emmeline Press, 1976); Vicky Burgess-Olson, ed., *Sister Saints* (Provo, Utah: BYU Press, 1978); Leonard J. Arrington, "Blessed Damozels: Women in Mormon History," *Dialogue: A Journal of Mormon Thought* 6 (Summer 1971), 22–31; Arrington, "Blessed Relief Society Sisters," in Maren M. Mouritsen, ed., *Blueprints for Living: Perspectives for Latter-day Saint Women* (Provo, Utah: Brigham Young University, 1980), 2:14–24; Beecher and Anderson, *Sisters in Spirit*; and Derr et al., *Women of Covenant*.

6. The standard biography is Carol Cornwall Madsen, "A Mormon Woman in Victorian America," (PhD diss., University of Utah, 1985); published as Madsen, *An Advocate for Women: The Public Life of Emmeline B. Wells, 1870–1920* (Salt Lake City: Deseret Book Co./Provo, Utah: BYU Press, 2006); also Madsen, *Emmeline B. Wells: An Intimate History* (Salt Lake City: University of Utah Press, 2017). Short biographies include Carol Cornwall Madsen, "Emmeline B. Wells: Romantic Rebel," in Donald O. Cannon and David J. Whittaker, eds., *Supporting Saints: Life Stories of Nineteenth-Century Mormons* (Provo, Utah: Brigham Young University, 1985), 305–41; Janet Peterson and LaRene Gaunt, "Emmeline B. Wells," in *Elect Ladies* (Salt Lake City: Deseret Book Co., 1990), 79–94; Patricia Rasmussen Eaton-Gadsby and Judith Rasmussen Dushku, "Emmeline B. Wells," in Burgess-Olson, *Sister Saints*, 457–78; Augusta Joyce Crocheron, "Emmeline B. Wells," in *Representative Women of Deseret* (Salt Lake City: Privately published, 1884), 62–71; Andrew Jenson, "Wells, Emmeline Blanche Woodward," in *Latter-day Saints Biographical Encyclopedia*, 4 vols. (Salt Lake City: Andrew Jenson History Company, 1898–1936), 2:731–34, 4:199–200; Orson F. Whitney, "Emmeline B. Woodward Wells," in *History of Utah*, 4 vols. (Salt Lake City: George Q. Cannon & Sons, 1892–1904), 4:586–90; and Susa Young Gates, "Emmeline B. Wells," in *History of the Young Ladies' Mutual Improvement Association*, Rev. (Salt Lake City: General Board of the Y.L.M.I.A., 1911), 45–53. See also Rebecca Anderson, "Emmeline B. Wells: Her Life and Thought," (master's thesis, Utah State University, 1975).

Emmeline B. Wells

when Emmeline was four, was in the War of 1812. A precocious child, Emmeline attended local schools, then was sent to a boarding school in New Salem, Massachusetts. During her absence, her mother joined the Mormon church. When Emmeline returned from school in 1842, she was baptized in an ice covered pool on their farm on her fourteenth birthday. She taught school for a year in Orange, Massachusetts, and then at the urging of her mother, who worried that she might succumb to the pressure of her friends and superiors to give up Mormonism, she married James Harris, the son of the local LDS branch president. She was fifteen, James was sixteen. They traveled by steamboat on the Mississippi River, arriving in March 1844. Emmeline wrote:

> At last the boat reached the upper landing, and a crowd of people were coming toward the bank of the river. As we stepped ashore the crowd advanced, and I could see one person who towered away

and above all the others around him. ... His majestic bearing so entirely different from anyone I had ever seen ... was more than a surprise. It was as if I beheld a vision. Before I was aware of it he came to me, and when he took my hand, I was simply electrified—thrilled through and through to the tips of my fingers, and every part of my body, as if some magic elixir had given me new life and vitality. ... The one thought that filled my soul was, "I have seen the prophet of God, he has taken me by the hand."[7]

Just two months later, this man, Joseph Smith, and his brother Hyrum were killed in the Carthage, Illinois, jail.

"Emmie," as she was called at the time, taught grade school and Sunday school in Nauvoo. She gave birth to a son who died within a month. Shortly after, her husband left her, never to return. Emmeline was befriended by Elizabeth Ann Whitney (1800–82), wife of the church's Presiding Bishop Newel K. Whitney (1795–1850) and a counselor to Emma Smith in the Relief Society, who took Emmeline into her household. Emmeline became Whitney's plural wife in 1845; he was fifty, she was almost seventeen. After the exodus west from Nauvoo, Emmeline taught school and Sunday school in Winter Quarters, Nebraska.

Many years later, Emmeline learned that James Harris had never remarried and had died in 1859 in Bombay, India, while working on a whaling vessel. He had written many letters to her but mailed them to his mother who had not forward them to Emmeline. On a trip to New England after the death of Harris's mother in 1888, Emmeline visited his childhood home. While rummaging through the attic, she came across the letters. Emmeline insisted that her daughter and granddaughter, who were with her, take her to the cemetery. Her granddaughter wrote of the event, "There that tiny but mighty old lady stood with her arms raised over the grave and

---

7. *Young Woman's Journal* 16 (December 1905): 554–56.

called down a curse upon her mother-in-law that made Mother tremble—and no doubt caused the wicked one to writhe in her shroud."[8] However much Emmeline suffered from the loss of her first husband and first child, she had the love and friendship of Bishop Whitney's first wife, Elizabeth Ann, a gracious, thoughtful, and generous person.

The Whitneys arrived in the Salt Lake Valley in October 1848, and a month and a half later Emmeline's eldest daughter was born in a wagon in the Whitney block, just north and west of Temple Square in downtown Salt Lake City. Emmeline returned to teaching, this time in a small log schoolhouse in Salt Lake City's LDS Twelfth Ward. As she recalled of this teaching experience:

> I taught 65 children in a log house without desks, charts, blackboards, or scarcely two books of the same kind. The remuneration was likewise trying, [one] bringing a piece of salt pork, another a bucket of flour, third perhaps a skein of yarn; to repay the ever toiling task of school teaching, the work was unceasing; the day spent in the school room and the night in planning and working on bits of cardboard mottoes in various colored silks for rewards, to urge the children to diligence and good behavior.[9]

Emmeline had two children by Whitney before he died on September 24, 1850. With his death, she suffered another period of anguish. Four years later, she wrote to one of Whitney's close friends, Daniel H. Wells (1814–91), and asked him to consider her lonely state. Wells married her as a plural wife in 1852, and Emmeline had three additional daughters by him. Wells, a prominent Salt Lake City businessman, superintendent of public works for the LDS Church, and later a counselor to Brigham Young in the First Presidency, provided her with a home and some income, paid for

---

8. Madsen, "A Mormon Woman in Victorian America," 78.

9. *Woman's Exponent* 17 (June 1, 1888): 1–2.

the education of her five daughters, and allowed her to concentrate on her reading, writing, and public speaking, as well as afforded her a prominent place in the community. While her children were small, however, Emmeline was devoted almost exclusively to her home and family. She worked in her garden, sang in the choir of the Old Tabernacle, wrote verses, and visited with friends.

Wells was a small woman, barely five feet tall, and weighed about a hundred pounds. Refusing to wear black dresses or a veil over her face, she wore pastel colors and soft, flowing scarves at her neck. But she had a supreme will. As Susa Young Gates described Wells when she was ninety, "Our little, delicate, great-minded President of the Relief Society, walked softly, yet with fierce independence into the room."[10] Wells expressed her goal as follows: "I desire to do all in my power to help elevate the condition of my people, especially women ... to do those things that would advance women in moral and spiritual, as well as educational work and tend to the rolling on of the work of the Lord upon the earth."[11]

In 1869, when Brigham Young organized the Young Ladies' Retrenchment Association, with Eliza Snow as president, Wells began to serve as Snow's private secretary, a position she held for the next six years. Clearly, she absorbed some of Snow's wisdom and gift for organization.

Impressed with the importance of providing cultural development for young people along literary and musical lines, Wells joined with others to organize the Wasatch Literary Association, considered by many to be the parent of the Young Ladies' and Young Men's Mutual Improvement Associations. Formed in 1874 by thirty young Salt Lake City persons, nearly all practicing Latter-day

---

10. Susa Young Gates, "Our Lovely Human Heritage," *Relief Society Magazine* 4 (February 1917): 74.

11. Emmeline B. Wells, Diary, January 4, 1878, 207, L. Tom Perry Special Collections, Harold B. Lee Library, Brigham Young University, Provo, Utah.

Saints, the Literary Association met weekly in the Wells and other homes. They composed and presented essays, poems, orations, plays and dramatic readings, vocal and instrumental musical renditions, and socialized. They studied and demonstrated creativity in general literature, music, and drama. Two of the sixty who belonged from 1874 to 1878 became LDS Church apostles, one was Utah's first elected governor, one became head of the Christian Science Church in Boston, one became Utah's first general in the US Army, one became president of the LDS Church, and several were LDS stake presidents. One became senior president of the church's First Quorum of Seventy, and one served twenty-four years as president of the Primary Association of the church.[12] With Wells's assistance and encouragement, these high-spirited future leaders fostered as much culture as their theocracy and pioneer economy permitted.

Although Wells was not at the 1842 meeting at which Joseph Smith delivered the keys to women, she was, as noted, a close friend and confidante of Elizabeth Anne Whitney, who had not only been at the meeting but had served as second counselor to Emma Smith and later to Eliza Snow. Wells also met frequently with the "leading sisters" in Winter Quarters, Nebraska, before the trek to Salt Lake Valley. As the plural wife of Newel Whitney and then of Daniel Wells, she formed close friendships with Snow, Bathsheba W. Smith, Zina D. H. Young, Mary Isabella Horne, Jane S. Richards, Sarah M. Kimball, Helen Mar Kimball Whitney, and other LDS women leaders, all of whom shared an interest in the cause of women. As an educated product of Massachusetts schools, Wells read national newspapers and magazines and, as she reared her children, watched with mounting interest the formation of a female reform movement aimed at social, educational, economic, and political equality with men. Wells had probably seen *Vindication*

12. Ronald W. Walker, "Growing Up in Early Utah: The Wasatch Literary Association, 1874–1878," *Sunstone* 6 (November–December 1981): 44–51.

of the Rights of Woman (1792) by the English author Mary Woll-stonecraft, a plain-spoken attack on the sexist conventions of the day. She also knew of the efforts of Massachusetts women, particu-larly Abigail Adams, who agitated for women's rights in the federal constitution, and had probably read Margaret Fuller's American Feminist statement, *Woman in the Nineteenth Century,* published in 1845. Wells also read of the first woman's rights convention in Seneca Falls, New York, which Elizabeth Cady Stanton organized in 1848. That meeting launched the woman's suffrage movement.[13] In 1874, Wells became vice president for Utah at the National Wom-an's Suffrage Association. With her children now adults and "out of the house," she embraced "public duties."

As Wells knew, there were good reasons for these movements. Women could not vote, hold office, sit on juries, or, if married, own property unless by special dispensation; women were not ex-pected to hold high positions in church, go to college, practice law, or speak in public.[14] Wells rejoiced when Utah women were given the vote in 1870 and began immediately, eagerly, to exercise her prerogatives. She became a member of the Central Committee of the People's Party, the LDS Church's political party; was a member of several constitutional conventions when Utah was attempting to become a state; and was nominated for the territorial legislature but was forced to withdraw when it was not clear from the constitution that women could hold elective office. In 1879, she experienced first-hand discrimination when she was denied the office of Salt Lake City treasurer because she was a woman.

From the time she was a teenager in school, Wells had written

---

13. Madsen, "A Mormon Woman in Victorian America," 148. See also Elea-nor Flexner, *A Century of Struggle: The Woman's Rights Movement in America,* rev. ed. (Cambridge, Massachusetts: The Belknap Press, 1975); and Eleanor Flexner, *Mary Wollstonecraft* (Baltimore: Penguin Books Inc., 1973).

14. Anne Firor Scott, "Mormon Women, Other Women: Paradoxes and Chal-lenges," *Journal of Mormon History* 13 (1986–87): 4.

poetry and had even published verses when she was in Nauvoo. She wrote the poem "Our Mountain Home So Dear," which Evan Stephens (1854–1930) later set to music and which continues to be a favorite LDS hymn.[15] A devoted gardener, Wells also wrote poems about flowers, plants, and gardening. In 1872, when the *Woman's Exponent* was founded by Louisa Lula Greene, under the careful tutelage and protection of Eliza R. Snow and Brigham Young, Wells submitted material for it, often using the pen name, "Blanche Beechwood." Many of her articles dealt with women's issues—equal pay for equal work, even equality in athletic programs.

After Lula Greene married Levi Richards and began to have children, her work on the *Exponent* slackened and Wells stepped forward as assistant editor. In 1877, she became editor, a position she held until 1914, when the *Exponent* was replaced by the *Relief Society Magazine*. In the *Exponent,* Wells recorded the national story of woman's suffrage, the silk industry, the wheat-storing project, and other activities of the Relief Societies, literary and other club functions, and welfare organizations and educational institutions. She commented on slavery, polygamy, European diplomacy, Congressional reform, and presidential elections. If it happened to women, whether locally, nationally, or overseas, Wells reported it in the *Exponent,* believing that LDS women "should be the best-informed of any women on the face of the earth, not only upon our own principles and doctrines but on all general subjects."[16]

Through the *Exponent,* Wells set out to replace the widely held belief that LDS women were debased and suppressed, instead projecting on the pages of the publication a positive image of intelligence, boldness, competence, and self-assurance. For more than

---

15. Wells, *Musings and Memories* (Salt Lake City: George Q. Cannon & Sons, 1896), 145–46.

16. Emmeline B. Wells, Letter to Mary Elizabeth Lightner, April 7, 1882, Wells Papers, LDS Church History Library.

twenty years, the masthead carried the motto "The Rights of the Women of Zion and the Rights of the Women of All Nations." At the Jubilee (50th) celebration of the Relief Society in Salt Lake City in 1892, Wells (writing as Blanche Beechwood) exulted: "Not only that fifty years ago this organization was founded by a Prophet of God, but that woman is becoming emancipated from error and superstition and darkness. That light has come into the world, and the Gospel has made her free, that the key of knowledge has been turned, and she has drank inspiration at the divine fountain."[17]

Wells campaigned against "The Cult of True Womanhood" of the period: "See the manner in which ladies—a term for which I have little reverence or respect—are treated in all public places: … She must be preserved from the slightest blast of trouble, petted, caressed, dressed to attract attention, taught accomplishments that minister to man's gratification; in other words, she must be treated as a glittering and fragile toy, a thing without brains or soul, placed on a tinselled and unsubstantial pedestal by man, as her worshipper."[18]

On October 1, 1874, the *Exponent* ran an article by Wells (again as Blanche Beechwood) that asked,

> Is there nothing then worth living for, but to be petted, humored and caressed, by a man? That is all very well as far as it goes, but that man is the only thing in existence worth living for I fail to see. All honor and reverence to good men; but they and their attentions are not the only sources of happiness on the earth, and need not fill up every thought of woman. And when men see that women exist without their being constantly at hand, that they can learn to be

---

17. *Woman's Exponent* 20 (April 15, 1892): 144.

18. Qtd. in the article on Wells in Richard S. Van Wagoner and Steven C. Walker, *A Book of Mormons* (Salt Lake City: Signature Books, 1982), 384. The most complete description of the meaning of the phrase is Barbara Welter, "The Cult of True Womanhood: 1800–1860," *American Quarterly* 18 (1966): 151–74.

self-reliant or depend upon each other for more or less happiness, it will perhaps take a little of the conceit out of some of them.[19]

A man too often saw his wife as "simply a necessity in his establishment," Wells observed, "… to manage his house, to cook his dinner, to attend to his wardrobe, always on hand if she is wanted and always out of sight when not needed. He doesn't mind kissing her occasionally, when it suits him; but he never thinks she has any thoughts of her own, any ideas which might be developed; she must not have even an opinion, or if she has she mustn't express it, it is entirely out of place; she is a subject, not a joint-partner in the domestic firm."

If men are really superior to women, let them show themselves so; prove themselves "pre-eminent," "akin to God." To Wells, a satisfying marriage was one in which both partners supported and uplifted the other.[20]

Indeed, through the pages of *Exponent,* Wells called for women to be given the same educational opportunities as men:

> … is it not time that after long years of bitter experience, some of us should learn that there is a better part for women than to be man's dupe, or slave, or drudge? Will mothers ever learn that the training of daughters as well as sons should be such as to develop powers that will strengthen character, attributes that will prepare them to put into practical execution the finest talents they may possess, so that they may learn how to live without leaning wholly on, or trusting blindly to another? It seems to me to be wholly and radically wrong when girls, even women, marry for a livelihood, marry because they are not practical enough to earn their own bread, instead at choosing their partner to add to the sum of human happiness, and the higher development of womanhood. …

---

19. "Why, Ah! Why," *Woman's Exponent* 3 (October 1, 1874): 67. In the next few paragraphs, I depend heavily on the analysis of Carol Cornwall Madsen, "Emmeline B. Wells: Romantic Rebel," in which many of these quotations are found.

20. "Real Women," *Woman's Exponent* 2 (January 1, 1874): 118.

In the name of justice, reason, and common sense, let woman be fortified and strengthened by every possible advantage, that she may be adequately and thoroughly fitted not only to grace the drawing room, and manage every department of her household, but to perform with skill and wisdom the arduous and elaborate work of molding and fashioning the fabrics of which society is to be woven.[21]

If women were given the same opportunities for work and for education as men, Wells insisted, they would demonstrate that they were as smart as men, as able as men to exercise leadership in social, religious, and business activities. The desirable goal was for men and women to work together, to be united, to share both responsibilities and ideas.[22]

Wells was not contending that women should neglect their children in seeking to do "public work." She had a close relationship with her own daughters—Belle, Mellie, Emmie, Annie, and Louie—mentioning them almost daily in her diary. But she insisted that women should also be free to assume responsibilities outside the home—in church, in the community, and in the world of business:

It is the opinion of many who are wise and learned that woman's mission upon the earth is maternity, with its minor details, its accompanying cares and anxieties, and needful exigencies; that these fill the measure of her creation; and when this is done, she should with becoming matronly dignity, retire from the sphere of active life and gracefully welcome old age. That motherhood brings into a woman's life a richness, zest and tone that nothing else ever can I gladly grant you, but that her usefulness ends there, or that she has no other individual interests to serve I cannot so readily concede.[23]

---

21. "After Long Years," *Woman's Exponent* 6 (November 15, 1877): 89; 4 (May 15, 1876): 191.

22. See also Orson F. Whitney, "Woman's Work and Mormonism," *Young Woman's Journal* 17 (July 1906): 295–96.

23. "Life Lessons, by Blanche Beechwood," *Woman's Exponent* 4 (October 1, 1875): 70.

Wells found herself juggling family and personal challenges with her work with the *Woman's Exponent,* the women's suffrage movement, and the Relief Society.[24]

Two specific assignments given to Wells in the late 1870s evolved into lifetime responsibilities. In 1876, Brigham Young asked her to lead a churchwide grain storage program. The Relief Society sisters gleaned from the fields, built their own granaries, and distributed grain to thousands of poor families to eat, feed to livestock, and plant. Supplies were also shipped to victims of national disasters and war in San Francisco, China, Turkey, and elsewhere. The program continued until World War I, when the 100,000 bushels the sisters had accumulated were sold by LDS Presiding Bishop Charles W. Nibley to the US government for distribution overseas during World War I. US President Woodrow Wilson, on a brief visit to Salt Lake City, visited Wells in her apartment in the Hotel Utah, and thanked her for this contribution to the American war effort.[25]

In 1870, LDS leaders encouraged Wells and Zina Young Williams to attend the meeting of the National Woman's Suffrage Association in Washington, DC; Relief Society leaders continued to take an active role in that association until the passage of the national women suffrage law in 1920. National leaders respected and admired the LDS women leaders, and the high regard was reciprocated. Wells wore a gold ring Susan B. Anthony gave to her, declaring, "It is a symbol of the sympathy of two great women for one great cause."[26] On Anthony's eightieth birthday, Wells presented her with a black brocaded dress made from Utah silk. Wells formed close friendships with other national women leaders: Frances E. Willard, Elizabeth Cady Stanton, Anna Howard Shaw,

---

24. *Elect Ladies,* 85, where the preceding quotations also appear.

25. See especially Jessie Embry, "Relief Society Grain Storage Program, 1876–1940," (master's thesis, Brigham Young University, 1974).

26. Anderson, "Emmeline B. Wells: Her Life and Thought," 33.

Sarah Andrews Spencer, Lucy Stone, Julia Ward Howe, May Wright Sewall, Clara Barton, Matilda Joslyn Gage, and others.

On her 1888 visit to New England and the East in connection with suffrage work, Wells spent one day with John Greenleaf Whittier, who years before had written sympathetically about the Latter-day Saints; she had an interview with Rose Elizabeth Cleveland, sister of US President Grover Cleveland who presided as Cleveland's hostess in the White House; she dined with Lucy Stone, and had tea with Elizabeth Stuart Phelps Ward, a Massachusetts resident who was widely acclaimed for her religious fiction and spiritual poetry.

In 1891, Wells went to Washington, DC, with Jane S. Richards to attend the first session of the National Council of Women. At that time, the council accepted the Relief Society as a charter member of the feminist organization.

At the World's Congress of Women, held in Chicago at the Columbian Exposition in 1893, Wells was a prominent figure and presided at one of the important council meetings. Largely because of her efforts as chair of the women of Salt Lake County in preparing for the event, non-LDS, Jewish, and Mormon women united in making a creditable showing at the exposition. May Wright Sewall, national chair of the Congress of Women, recognized the importance of the Relief Society and Young Ladies' Mutual Improvement Association and used her influence to arrange department meetings for them in connection with the congress. At the Relief Society session, Wells gave papers on "Western Women in Journalism" and "The Storage of Grain." Wells also edited two books exhibited in the Utah Pavilion: *Charities and Philanthropies: Woman's Work in Utah* and *Songs and Flowers of the Wasatch*, both published in 1893 by George Q. Cannon & Sons.

In the years that followed, Wells attended suffrage conventions and women's congresses in Washington, DC, Omaha, New Orleans,

Des Moines, Atlanta, Detroit, Chicago, Indianapolis, and London, and addressed several of them. At the National Council held in Washington in 1895, she read a paper on "Forty years in the Valley of the Great Salt Lake," which was reproduced in many leading newspapers and magazines. At the Atlanta convention held later that year, she delivered an address dealing with Utah and the LDS people. So well was her talk received that, at its conclusion, the auditorium resounded with tumultuous applause and Susan B. Anthony came forward on the rostrum and embraced her. She also received hearty approval in Utah.

In June 1899, as an officer of the National Council of Women (she was recording secretary 1899–1902), Wells attended and was a speaker at the international Council and Congress of Women held in London. She presented her address in Convocation Hall, Church House, Deanery of Westminster Abbey, London. She visited historic places while in England, Scotland, and France, and spent an evening with popular author Marie Corelli at Stratford-on-Avon. Among the select guests who were received by Queen Victoria, she also formed friendships with the Duchess of Sutherland, the Princess Gabrielle Wiszniewska, Duchess De Luynes, Adeline D. T. Whitney, and Lady Aberdeen.

Wells also advanced in responsibility on the LDS Church scene. In 1888, she became general secretary and a member of the general board of the Relief Society, and assisted in the organization of the Young Ladies' Mutual Improvement Association and Primary Association.

On October 3, 1910, after twenty-two years of service on the general level of Relief Society, Wells was called to be the fifth general president of the organization, succeeding her long-time friend Bathsheba W. Smith. She named Clarissa Smith Williams and Julina Lambson Smith as her counselors. She was eighty-two. She continued as president until 1921, when she was ninety-two. Under her leadership, she standardized and systematized the work of the Relief Society, instituted the *Relief Society Magazine*, began the first uniform course of study, and adopted the slogan "Charity Never Faileth." Welfare work became more methodical, and she coordinated Relief Society work with those of civic and county agencies. In 1919, a social services department was organized under the direction of Amy Brown Lyman. Under Wells's leadership the Relief Society also established courses in theology, genealogy, art, and literature, while courses on obstetrics, nursing, "home science," and home arts were continued. Each LDS ward and stake, however, was encouraged to work out its own program.

Wells also founded the Utah Woman's Press Club and Reapers' Club and published a book of her poetry entitled *Musings and Memories* (1896). A second edition, including her later poems and some not previously published, was printed in 1915.

In recognition of Wells's many efforts and achievements in literature, Brigham Young University, in 1912, conferred upon her, on her eighty-fourth birthday, the honorary degree of Doctor of Letters. She was the second person to receive the honor and the first woman. BYU would wait forty-four years before honoring another woman in this way.

About that time, Susa Young Gates wrote of her: "Emmeline's mind is keen, her intellect sure, and her powers unbending. She possesses a rarely beautiful spirit, and is affectionate, confiding and exquisitely pure. No unclean thing could enter her presence, or remain in her atmosphere. She is an eloquent speaker, a beautiful writer, a true friend, and a wise counsellor. She is beloved by all who dwell in the Church, and by all who know her, and their name is legion."[27]

When Wells turned ninety, a party was given for her at the Hotel Utah. To mark the occasion, a motion picture was made of her and

---

27. Susa Young Gates, "President Emmeline B. Wells," *Album Book: Daughters of the Utah Pioneers and Their Mothers,* ed. Joseph T. Jakeman (Salt Lake City: Daughters of Utah Pioneers, 1911), 54.

other pioneers who had lived in Nauvoo during the time Joseph Smith was alive. On her ninety-second birthday, more than a thousand people attended her birthday party in the Hotel Utah.[28]

Prior to Wells's death, Susa Young Gates, her associate on the general board of the Relief Society for many years, wrote of her:

> She has been a living encyclopaedia of information on all subjects connected with the cause of woman, both historical and civil. She has been and is a bureau of information for every association, society and club in the state. It is a liberal education to listen to her conversation, and she is possessed of some of the rarest traits ever given to woman. She is sensitive without smallness, she is wise without narrowness, and religious without bigotry. She is a tender, loving link between the women of the Church and those without, both of whom reverence and love her for the good she has done. She is sarcastic at times, not to say caustic, but her repentance follows swift on the heels of her offence.[29]
>
> The most unusual and delightful trait about Mrs. Wells is her keen sense of humor; this power has prolonged her life and preserved her reason, in the midst of crushing trials, while it makes her a delightful companion to men and women alike. If one were to sum up in one word the deepest impression given by this remarkable woman, it would be done in that elusive term "refinement." She is exquisitely delicate and dainty, in her writing, her living, and in her life. Such, briefly, is the woman who is an inspiration to her friends, a thorn to her envious associates, and a "companion of princes" in her own right.[30]

Shortly after her release from the presidency of the Relief Society, Wells died, age ninety-three. Her funeral was in the Tabernacle in Salt Lake City, the second funeral ever held in that Temple Square

---

28. *Elect Ladies*, 90.

29. Orson F. Whitney wrote that Wells could be "frank and outspoken almost to bluntness" (*History of Utah* 4:586).

30. Gates, *History of the Y.L.W.I.A.*, 52–53.

facility for a woman. (The first was for Bathsheba Smith, who was Wells's predecessor as general president of the Relief Society.)

On Wells's 100th anniversary, seven years after her death, the women of Utah placed a bust of her in the rotunda of the Utah State Capitol Building; the brief inscription reads, "A fine soul who served us."

o o o

Other significant women who were leaders of faith and intellect at the turn of the twentieth century include Susa Young Gates and Alice Merrill Horne.

Gates (1856–1933) was the second daughter of Brigham Young and Lucy Bigelow, and the first child born in the Lion House in downtown Salt Lake City.[31] Educated in her father's private school, by the age of fourteen she had also received a practical education and was considered capable as a stenographer and as a telegrapher. In 1877, she not only took down the ceremonies for the dedication of the newly completed LDS St. George, Utah, temple, but was the first person to be baptized there for the dead. While attending the University of Deseret, Susa launched the first college literary journal in the West. She was the first Mormon to write a novel of Mormon life and published other novels, biographies, manuals, and hundreds of articles for national and local magazines. She also founded and edited the *Young Woman's Journal* (1889–1929).

In 1878, Susa taught music at Brigham Young Academy (later Brigham Young University). Two years later, she married Jacob F. Gates, and the two served a proselyting mission in Hawaii. She was the first woman to accompany her husband on such an assignment. Returning to the Brigham Young Academy, she organized the

---

31. Articles on Gates's life include Carolyn W. D. Person, "Susa Young Gates," in Bushman, *Mormon Sisters*, 198–223; and Rebecca Foster Cornwall, "Susa Young Gates: The Thirteenth Apostle," in Burgess-Olson, *Sister Saints*, 61–93. See also Paul Cracroft, "Susa Young Gates: Her Life and Her Work," (master's thesis, University of Utah, 1959).

Susa Young Gates   *Alice Merrill Horne*

domestic (home economics) department in 1897. Besides teaching theology, music, and domestic science, she bore thirteen children, seven of whom died in childhood accidents or illnesses. Some of them achieved distinction, including Emma Lucy Gates, an internationally renowned soprano. An active suffragette, Susa was also an officer and delegate to the National and International Council of Women, a long-time officer of the Young Ladies' Mutual Improvement Association and the Relief Society, and editor of the *Relief Society Magazine* from 1914 to 1933.

With an office in the Church Administration Building, she was jokingly referred to as "the thirteenth apostle." A favorite admonition of hers was, "Provoke the brethren to good works, but don't provoke the brethren while you are doing so."[32]

Another compatriot of this period was Alice Merrill Horne, born in a log cabin in Fillmore, Utah, on January 2, 1868, the fourth of fourteen children born to Clarence and Bathsheba Smith Merrill.[33]

---

32. Qtd. in Van Wagoner and Walker, *A Book of Mormons,* 91.

33. Harriet Horne Arrington and Leonard J. Arrington, "Alice Merrill Horne, Cultural Entrepreneur," in Mary E. Stovall and Carol Cornwall Madsen, eds., *A Heritage of Faith* (Salt Lake City: Deseret Book Co., 1988), 131–36; and Robert S. Olpin, *Dictionary of Utah Art* (Salt Lake City: Salt Lake Art Center, 1980), 126–28.

She began school at the Old Rock Schoolhouse in Fillmore, but at the age of nine went to Salt Lake City to live with her recently widowed grandmother, Bathsheba (Mrs. George A.) Smith. After completing grade school, she attended the University of Deseret (later the University of Utah) where she graduated in 1887 with a degree in pedagogy. She was especially interested in art, education, literature, and writing. She married George H. Horne, a Salt Lake City banker, and subsequently bore six children. George Horne died in 1934.

Alice first taught school in Fillmore. While George was on a mission for the LDS Church to the Southern States, she taught at Washington School in Salt Lake City, and continued as an educator during the ensuing years.

Alice studied art at the University of Deseret, the Art Institute in Chicago, and privately under J. T. Harwood, John Hafen, Herman Haag, Mary Teasdel, and Henry Taggart. She became closely associated with many prominent Intermountain artists. Lee Green Richards dedicated a portrait of Bathsheba Smith to "Mother Horne," the name by which Alice was referred to by the artists.

In 1891, only twenty-three years old, Alice Horne was appointed chair of the Utah Liberal Arts Committee for the 1893 Columbian Exposition in Chicago, for which she published a book of poems written by Utah women poets and illustrated by women artists in Utah. She also supervised the preparation of various creations by Utah women that were exhibited in the Woman's Building in Chicago. Another focus of her exhibit on Utah literature and literary development centered on the extensive traveling library of the Y.W.M.I.A. which serviced Utah and Intermountain settlements.

In 1898, Horne was elected a member of the Utah House of Representatives, the second woman to serve in that body. She introduced and shepherded through a bill to create an art institute—a landmark bill which inaugurated the first art institute in the United States—to encourage the development of the fine arts in Utah (art, music, literature, and dance); to hold an annual art exhibition; and to initiate a state-owned art collection. In her honor, the state collection is called the Alice Art Collection. Alice also sponsored a law that provided four-year tuition-paid teaching scholarships to students at the University of Utah; and she served as chair of the University Land-Site committee that chose the present location of the University of Utah.

In 1901, Horne was made a member of the General Board of the National Women's Relief Society, and served on the board for fourteen years. As chair of the Relief Society's art committee, she prepared lessons on art appreciation, landscape study, and architecture that she published for use in their classes. She also contributed articles to the *Improvement Era, Juvenile Instructor, Relief Society Magazine,* and *Woman's Exponent.* As chair of the Infant Care Committee for the society, she also sponsored a "Clean Milk for Utah" campaign that resulted in more rigid inspection standards for milk sold in the state. As a part of this effort, she established four free milk stations in different parts of Salt Lake City for the benefit of undernourished and underprivileged babies.

In 1904, Horne represented the National Woman's Relief Society and the United States at the International Congress of Women in Berlin, Germany, and gave two addresses to the Congress: one on the Utah Art Movement, and the other on women in politics, recounting her experience as an elected woman legislator. She served for several years as Utah chair of the International Peace Committee. A charter member, she wrote the constitution of the Daughters of Utah Pioneers, was elected first secretary, historian, and second president, and participated in the organization of the Daughters of the Revolution in 1896, later filling the position of state regent.

Horne's most important contribution to Utah, however, was in art for which she is appreciatively known as the "First Lady of Utah Art." In the 1920s, 1930s, and 1940s, she promoted Intermountain artists by exhibiting and selling their paintings so "they could earn a livelihood" as artists. She advised art patrons, "In each home there should hang a good picture, no matter how small." She held art exhibitions throughout the state, especially in prominent locations in Salt Lake City, schools, universities, and public buildings. "If you really want to learn what art is, live with it; make it a part of your home and your experience," she advised. Determined that Utah children would have the advantage of original art around them, she sponsored thirty-seven art collections which were exhibited in the state's schools. She also wrote and published *Devotees and Their Shrines: A Handbook of Utah Art* (1914), the first book written on Utah Art and used extensively by the Relief Societies; an historic play for elementary schools, *Columbus Westward Ho!* (1922); and a periodical, *Art Strands*, that carried news on art in Utah during the 1930s and 1940s.

In the 1930s, she organized the "Smokeless Fuel Federation" to eliminate the environmental hazards of coal as a home-heating fuel, and was secretary of the Woman's Chamber of Commerce. In 1934, she was chosen by the Salt Lake Council of Women as one of the first outstanding women for her civic service, especially in the promotion of art appreciation and production.[34] Horne Hall, one of the Heritage Halls constructed in 1956 by Brigham Young University, was named for her.

Horne died of a heart attack on October 7, 1948, at the age of eighty.

To conclude, let us cite the statement of LDS historian Orson F. Whitney: "Among the outward evidence of the divine origin of 'Mormonism,' there is nothing that testifies more clearly or eloquently to the truth of the Latter-day work, than the provision made therein for the uplifting and advancement of woman; for the

---

34. Leah D. Widtsoe, "The Story of a Gifted Lady," *Relief Society Magazine* 32 (March 1945): 150–55.

salvation and exaltation, in this world and in the world to come, of woman as well as man."[35]

Advancement of the status of women began with the organization of the LDS Church in 1830, the formation of the Relief Society in 1842, and Joseph Smith's subsequent action in turning the heavenly key to women that they might have a better day. Women used their privileges, as they referred to them, in creating programs and building institutions that blessed them and the church as a whole. Many LDS women heard the prophetic voice, acted upon it, and made lives brighter for their sisters in the church and throughout the world.

---

35. *Young Woman's Journal* 17 (July 1906): 293.

CHAPTER 4

James E. Talmage, B. H. Roberts, and W. H. Chamberlin

ADVOCATES FOR EDUCATION

Setting the Stage

In addition to the LDS women who went east to study medicine in the 1870s and 1880s, Latter-day Saint men and women, particularly in the 1880s and 1890s, eagerly matriculated at eastern and midwestern universities to study law, physics, engineering, architecture, and other subjects. Most retained a strong allegiance to Mormonism through their university experience and returned to Utah full of new ideas and anxious to share them with their fellow Saints. For some of them, it was Mormonism's first confrontation with serious intellectual challenges.[1]

"The glory of God is intelligence," Joseph Smith had said (D&C 93:36). The LDS commitment to Truth was unmistakable. As Brigham Young put it: "Our religion embraces all truth and every fact in existence, no matter whether in heaven, earth, or hell. A fact is a fact [and] all truth issues forth from the Fountain of truth."[2] But

---

1. I have used a paper prepared by Davis Bitton and myself, entitled "Twentieth Century Mormon Thought." I am grateful to Bitton, who generously gave me permission to use material from that paper in connection with this chapter. Some of Bitton's thinking may have changed since the paper was written, so I take full responsibility for what is said. See also Thomas W. Simpson, *American Universities and the Birth of Modern Mormonism, 1867–1940* (Chapel Hill: University of North Carolina Press, 2016).

2. Sermon of May 14, 1871, *Journal of Discourses,* 26 Vols. (Liverpool, England: Latter-day Saints Booksellers Depot, 1854–86), 14:117 (hereafter JD).

from its inception, Mormonism also saw itself as a "practical religion." Its theology was "practical," and so would be its education. Young declared that "the religion of Jesus Christ is a matter-of-fact religion, and taketh hold of the every-day duties and realities of this life."[3] "Practical religion" was a popular theme in LDS magazines, manuals, and books, and there was some mistrust of the theoretical, speculative "philosophies of men." That there existed a certain tension between "practical" and "intellectualized" religion is not surprising. LDS prophets did not wish to "put down" either.

Education was a good thing, and knowledge highly desirable, but the pride that sometimes accompanied higher learning was to be carefully guarded against: "O the vainness, and frailties, and the foolishness of men!" cried a Book of Mormon prophet. "When they are learned they think they are wise, and they hearken not unto the counsel of God, for they set it aside, supposing they know of themselves, wherefore, their wisdom is foolishness and it profiteth them not. And they perish. But to be learned is good if they hearken unto the counsels of God" (2 Ne. 9:28–29).

Any anti-intellectual tendencies in Mormonism were influenced not only by the anti-clerical attitudes the Saints shared with much of evangelical Protestantism but also by the demands of pioneer life that privileged the practical over the theoretical, and by the unavailability of higher education in the Great Basin. The Saints struggled to provide the best possible education for their children, but throughout the nineteenth century there was a shortage of trained teachers.[4] Older children were often needed to help their mothers with younger children, to help with farm work, or to take

---

3. JD 11:133, August 1–10, 1865.

4. See Ernest L. Wilkinson, ed., *Brigham Young University: The First One Hundred Years*, 4 vols. (Provo, Utah: Brigham Young University Press, 1975–76), 1:3–50; and Leonard J. Arrington, "The Latter-day Saints and Public Education," *Southwestern Journal of Social Education* 7 (Spring–Summer 1977): 9–25.

the role of breadwinner when the father was on a mission or imprisoned, as a practicing polygamist, "for conscience sake." As a result, with the rest of the nation, LDS education rarely exceeded the elementary grades. Sensing this as an opportunity to "save" the Mormons, Protestant missions, after the completion of the transcontinental railroad in 1869, began to establish a number of high schools throughout the territory to wean young Saints away from the errors of their fathers and mothers by providing a free or low-cost "Christian education." Many LDS children attended, but in the end the Protestant missions were forced to admit the program was unsuccessful as a proselytizing venture.[5] LDS children, by and large, remained faithful to their upbringing. On the advanced level, the University of Utah, founded in 1850 as the University of Deseret, was revived in 1869. It offered opportunities for LDS young people, but as a territorial (and later state) institution of higher learning, it could not promulgate Mormonism.

Strongly believing in the importance of education, Brigham Young established Brigham Young Academy (1875) in Provo, Utah, and Brigham Young College in Logan (1877), and laid plans for a Young University in Salt Lake City.[6] A few years later, in 1888,

---

5. T. Edgar Lyon, "Evangelical Protestant Activities in Mormon Dominated Areas, 1865–1900," (PhD diss., University of Utah, 1962).

6. Property intended for Young University by Brigham Young was acquired from his heirs, a building was constructed and furnished, and James E. Talmage, president of the LDS College, was engaged to head the new institution, but the nationwide financial panic of 1893 abruptly cut off appropriations for church schools from the general fund. University of Utah officials approached the First Presidency, suggesting the church throw its support to the state institution rather than establish a competing school in the same city. The presidency of the university was offered to Talmage as assurance that it would not fall into the hands of unfriendly non-Mormons. With the encouragement of the First Presidency, Talmage accepted both the position and an endowed chair-professorship of geology. He served as president from 1894 to 1897 and as professor of geology until his call to the LDS apostleship in 1921. See D. Michael Quinn, "The Brief Career of Young University at Salt Lake City," *Utah Historical Quarterly* 41 (Winter 1973): 69–89.

incoming Church President Wilford Woodruff organized a Church Board of Education, founded the Latter-day Saint College (variously known as the Salt Lake Stake Academy and the Latter-day Saint University), and initiated an ambitious program under which each LDS stake was asked to establish its own academy. These academies were essentially high schools, although from the beginning the Brigham Young Academy in Provo and Brigham Young College in Logan also had a "normal" program for training teachers.[7] A number of promising students were given grants and loans to pursue degrees in the Midwest and East with the understanding that they would return to teach in the church education system.

James E. Talmage

One of the forerunners of this movement was James E. Talmage, a student of pioneer LDS educator Karl G. Maeser (1828–1901) at the Brigham Young Academy.[8] Talmage was born in 1862 in Hungerford, Berkshire, England, the first son and second child of

---

7. Karl Maeser, a Saxon school teacher who converted to the LDS Church in Dresden, became the first principal of the Brigham Young Academy (1876–92) and the first superintendent of LDS schools (1888–1901). Maeser combined the classic Prussian curriculum and regimen with Brigham Young's emphasis on practical, theologically sound schooling. As a teacher, Maeser was a disciplinarian with high academic standards; as an administrator, a hard-working leader determined to provide the best possible education in the face of financial adversity. See Douglas F. Tobler, "Karl G. Maeser's German Background, 1828–1856: The Making of Zion's Teacher," *BYU Studies* 17 (Winter 1977): 155–75; and Wilkinson, *Brigham Young University*, 1:77–209. See also A. LeGrand Richards, *Called to Teach: The Legacy of Karl G. Maeser* (Provo, Utah: BYU Religious Studies Center/Salt Lake City: Deseret Book Co., 2014).

8. John R. Talmage, *The Talmage Story* (Salt Lake City: Bookcraft, 1972); shorter biographies include those in Orson F. Whitney, *History of Utah*, 4 vols. (Salt Lake City: George Q. Cannon. & Sons, 1892–1904), 4:357–60; Andrew Jenson, *Latter-day Saint Biographical Encyclopedia*, 4 vols. (Salt Lake City: Andrew Jenson History Co., 1902–36), 3:787–89; and Richard S. Van Wagoner and Steven C. Walker, *A Book of Mormons* (Salt Lake City: Signature Books, 1982), 343–47. See also Dennis Rowley, "Fishing on the Kennet: The Victorian Boyhood of James E. Talmage, 1862–1876," *BYU Studies* 33 (Fall 1993): 480–520.

eight. He attended local Berkshire and Wiltshire schools and was the Oxford diocesan prize scholar when he was twelve. In 1873, his family converted to the LDS Church, and in 1876, when Talmage was thirteen, they immigrated to the United States and settled in Provo, Utah, where Talmage enrolled at Brigham Young Academy. After five years, he graduated with majors in English and science and a teaching certificate, first in his class. He was at once engaged to teach at the academy.

Eager to pursue a higher education in science, Talmage attended Lehigh and John Hopkins Universities, 1882–84, and returned to teach in Provo, serving as professor of chemistry and geology. While in Provo, he became an American citizen, Provo City councilman, alderman, justice of the peace, LDS stake high councilor, and stake Superintendent of Schools. He married Merry May Booth (1868–1944) in 1888, and the couple had eight children. Also in 1888, Talmage became principal of the BYA, replacing Maeser, but was quickly called by the church to serve as first president of the new Latter-day Saint College in Salt Lake City, 1888–93.

Impressed with his academic achievements and religious ortho-doxy, the LDS First Presidency commissioned Talmage to prepare a text in theology for use in church schools and religion classes. The book, *Articles of Faith*, was based on lectures delivered in 1893 and 1894 in the Assembly Hall in downtown Salt Lake City. The first lecture was attended by more than 500 people; the last, six months later, by nearly 1,300 people. After review by a committee of LDS Church general authorities and Church Board of Education members, *The Articles of Faith* was published in 1899 and has served as a standard LDS reference work to the present time.[9] The work is important as the first extensive statement of LDS doctrine and

---

9. Talmage, *The Articles of Faith* (Salt Lake City: Published by the Church, 1899). The main topics of the book are the thirteen short "Articles of Faith" written by Joseph Smith and others in 1842 from a pamphlet published earlier by Orson Pratt.

James E. Talmage

attitude in the post-1890 Manifesto period. A moderate, carefully reasoned work with scriptural support, *The Articles of Faith* continues to be a good introduction to basic LDS beliefs.

Meanwhile, Talmage was president of the University of Utah from 1894 to 1897, when he resigned to devote full time to the Deseret Chair of Geology, which he held until his resignation in 1907 to serve as a consulting mining geologist and engineer. He was awarded a PhD by Illinois Wesleyan University for non-resident work in 1896. He became a fellow of numerous scientific societies in Great Britain and the United States, including the Royal Microscopical Society of London, the Royal Society of Edinburgh, Royal Scottish Geographical Society, the Geological Society of London (and of America), the Philosophical Society of Great Britain, and the American Association for the Advancement of Science. In 1911, he was ordained an LDS Church apostle and became a member of the Council of Twelve. His scientific books included *First Book of Nature* (1888), *Domestic Science* (1891), *Tables for Blowpipe Determination of Minerals* (1899), and *The Great Salt Lake, Present and Past* (1900). His religious books, in addition to *The Articles of Faith*, included *The Story of "Mormonism"* (1907), *The Great Apostasy* (1909), *The House of the Lord* (1912), *Jesus the Christ* (1915), and *The Vitality of "Mormonism"* (1919). His connections with learned societies gave him a prestige among Latter-day Saints that was seldom equaled by any other LDS leader of thought. His talks were based on reason, and he defended science from irrational dogma. He died in 1933. The epitaph on his tombstone expresses his scholarly and religious perspective: "Within the Gospel of Jesus Christ There Is Room and Place for Every Truth Thus Far Learned by Man or Yet to Be Made Known."

Buoyed by Talmage's success, other students and teachers began to flock to out-of-state universities. Joseph M. Tanner (1859–1927), a BYA student named principal of the Brigham Young College in Logan in 1888, left that position in 1891 to study law at Harvard, and later became superintendent of LDS Church Schools. Tanner took some of his most promising students with him to Harvard, several of whom returned to teach at BYC. Among them was John A. Widtsoe (1872–1952), who graduated with highest honors in biochemistry and completed a PhD at the University of Goettingen in Germany. His *Joseph Smith As Scientist* (1908) supported the view that Smith was a prophet of both science and religion, anticipating the "modern" understanding of the nature of matter and even evolution.[10] Widtsoe, as we shall see, became president of Utah

---

10. Widtsoe's book was preceded by an eleven-part series on the subject in the LDS Church's *Improvement Era* magazine in 1903–04, including one on "The Law of Evolution." In 1904, BYA professor of composition Nels L. Nelson (1862–1946) published *Scientific Aspects of Mormonism*. The First Presidency loaned Nelson $800 to pay an eastern publishing house to put the book out, then circulated a letter throughout the church praising it. Like many other Latter-day Saints of the period,

State Agricultural College in 1907, president of the University of Utah in 1917, and an LDS Church apostle in 1921.

What was the relationship, if any, between LDS doctrine and scientific-technological progress? It was common for Latter-day Saints to say that since the Mormon Restoration "there has come into the world, almost imperceptibly, a more generally diffused and brighter spirit of intelligence than was known before [by which] men have been led to those great discoveries in the arts and sciences and in mechanics, which make our age so wonderful as an age of progress and enlightenment."[11]

Latter-day Saints desired to become leaders in the world's advancement. By the outbreak of World War I, many LDS leaders had received advanced degrees from large universities. These included two who were later members of the church's First Presidency (J. Reuben Clark Jr. and Stephen L Richards); five apostles (James E. Talmage, Stephen L. Richards, Richard R. Lyman, John A. Widtsoe, and Joseph F. Merrill); three members of the First Council of Seventy (Charles H. Hart, Levi Edgar Young, and Oscar A. Kirkham); five superintendents of church schools and commissioners of education (Horace H. Cummings, Adam S. Bennion, Joseph F. Merrill, John A. Widtsoe, and Franklin L. West); and, of course, presidents of the University of Utah, Brigham Young University, and Utah State Agricultural College.

Michigan became a popular law school for Latter-day Saints, beginning with James H. Moyle (1858–1946) in 1881. Moyle, who received his degree in 1885, was the first Mormon to have high office in the national government, serving as Assistant Secretary

---

Nelson linked secular ideas of evolution with Joseph Smith's doctrine of eternal progression. Turn-of-the-century Saints found scientific support for their religious beliefs, inducing many students to take up studies in the physical sciences.

11. B. H. Roberts, sermon of October 3, 1903, *LDS Conference Report, October 1903* (Salt Lake City: Church of Jesus Christ of Latter-day Saints, 1903), 72.

of the Treasury in the cabinet of US President Woodrow Wilson. Moyle was also a loyal churchman and helped demonstrate that education at an eastern university did not lessen the Mormon student's loyalty to his or her church.

Moyle was followed at Michigan in 1887 by Charles H. Hart (1866–1934), who helped to prepare Utah's constitution and became a member of the First Council of Seventy. The president of Michigan's Class of 1895 was Richard R. Lyman (1870–1963), an engineering student who went on to obtain a PhD from Cornell and who was called to the apostleship in 1918. His wife, Amy Brown Lyman (1872–1959), who studied at the University of Chicago and did volunteer work with Jane Addams at Hull House, later became General President of the LDS Relief Society. Benjamin Cluff Jr. (1858–1948) also graduated from Michigan (1886), and upon completing his master's degree there was named president of Brigham Young Academy/University. Don B. Colton (1876–1952), congressman from Utah (1920–32), and William H. King (1863–1949), Utah's senator from 1917 to 1941, were two other Latter-day Saints to obtain their LLBs from Michigan.

Equaling Michigan in popularity among LDS students was the University of Chicago. Amy Brown Lyman estimated that there were thirty Utah students with her in 1902, including Alice Louise Reynolds (1873–1938) who had graduated from the BYA in 1890, then studied at Michigan, Chicago, California, Columbia, Paris, and Queens College (London) between teaching assignments in English at BYU. Henry D. Moyle (1889–1963) and Stephen L. Richards (1879–1959), later members of the church's First Presidency, and Apostle Albert E. Bowen (1875–1953) all obtained their law degrees at Chicago. In addition, there were Franklin L. West (1885–1966), who had studied at Stanford before completing a PhD at Chicago in physics and later became LDS Church Commissioner of Education; Horace H. Cummings (1858–1937), who studied at Chicago and Columbia before serving thirteen years as General Superintendent of LDS Church Schools (1906–19); Harvey Fletcher (1884–1981), father of stereophonic sound; Ephraim E. Ericksen (1882–1967), professor of philosophy and dean at the University of Utah; and his colleague on the church's YMMIA General Board, Arthur L. Beeley (1890–1973), also dean of Social Work at the University of Utah.

At Columbia, Levi Edgar Young (1874–1963) of the First Council of Seventy obtained a master's degree in history. Apostle Adam S. Bennion (1886–1958) completed a master's degree there in 1912 and a PhD from the University of California, Berkeley, in 1923. Frederick J. Pack (1875–1938), who taught geology at the University of Utah and wrote a defense of evolution for Mormons (*Science and Belief in God,* 1924), obtained his PhD in 1906. Lyman L. Daines (1883–1941), dean of the School of Medicine at the University of Utah, completed his PhD at UCB and his MD at Rush Medical College. Apostle Joseph F. Merrill (1868–1952) studied at Michigan (1889–93), Cornell (1892), Chicago (1894), and completed a PhD in physics in 1899 at Johns Hopkins. Franklin S. Harris (1884–1960), president of Brigham Young University, finished his PhD at Cornell.

As these men and women completed their university studies and returned to Utah to begin their careers, often as teachers in the church system, many were called to positions on LDS general boards—Education, Young Men's and Young Women's MIA, Primary, Relief Society, and Sunday School. They wrote articles for church magazines and manuals for the Sunday school, MIA, and Relief Society. Gradually, higher education was enriching the intellectual atmosphere of LDS society.[12]

---

12. John A. Widtsoe, Joseph F. Merrill, and E. E. Ericksen are discussed in somewhat more detail later in this chapter.

B. H. Roberts

Of all the advocates of higher education among the Latter-day Saints, none was more enthusiastic or optimistic than Brigham Henry (B. H.) Roberts.[13] A poor immigrant from England, Roberts walked across the plains to Utah at the age of nine. Born in Warrington, Lancashire, England, in 1857, Roberts was named for Brigham Young by his mother, who had just joined the LDS Church. Wife of an alcoholic, she took two of her children and went to Salt Lake City, leaving five-year-old Brigham and his older sister behind. Brigham was not well cared for, and wandered the streets as a poverty-stricken, unshepherded Dickensian ragamuffin for four years until, at age nine, he was able to cross the ocean and walk, reportedly barefoot, to Utah.

Settling with his mother in a one-room cabin in Centerville, north of Salt Lake City, Roberts began life as a farmhand, then as a construction worker. At age fourteen, he joined mining camps in western Utah, where he spent evenings in gambling, learning to drink, swear, and carouse. Warned that he was on his way to hell, he returned to Centerville, apprenticed himself to a blacksmith (his father's trade), and attended the University of Deseret, walking twelve miles daily.

An avid learner, he graduated within three years at the top of his Normal School class and gave the valedictory address. He married,

---

13. The standard references are Truman G. Madsen, *Defender of the Faith: The B. H. Roberts Story* (Salt Lake City: Bookcraft, 1980); B. H. Roberts, *The Autobiography of B. H. Roberts,* Gary James Bergera, ed. (Salt Lake City: Signature Books, 1990); John R. Sillito, ed., *History's Apprentice: The Diaries of B. H. Roberts, 1880–1898* (Salt Lake City: Signature Books, 2004); and Richard C. Roberts, *A History of the B. H. Roberts Family* (N.p.: N.p., 2009). See also Robert H. Malan, *B. H. Roberts: A Biography* (Salt Lake City: Deseret Book Co., 1966); Davis Bitton, "B. H. Roberts as an Historian," *Dialogue: A Journal of Mormon Thought* 3 (Winter 1968): 25–44; Leonard J. Arrington, "The Intellectual Tradition of Mormon Utah," *Proceedings of the Utah Academy of Sciences, Arts & Letters* 45 (1968): 1–20: and Brigham D. Madsen, ed., *The Essential B. H. Roberts* (Salt Lake City: Signature Books, 1999).

B. H. Roberts

taught school, and plied his trade as a blacksmith until 1880, when he was sent on a proselytizing mission to the Southern States.

Roberts became president of the mission in 1883, when he was only twenty-six. He was then sent as a missionary to England, where he served two years as editor of the *Latter-day Saints' Millennial Star.* After his return, he became a journalist, serving briefly as editor of the *Salt Lake Herald.* In 1888, at the age of thirty-one, he was sustained to the church's Council of Seventy, eventually becoming the senior president. He was an effective, vigorous missionary. Having developed his speaking ability in the South, he was one of the church's great orators. Preston Nibley (1884–1965), who watched him preach many times, described his style:

> How often have we seen him arise and face an audience, beginning at first to talk in a modulated tone, so low that he could scarcely be heard, increasing gradually in volume, making a point here and

there, and then upon reaching his climax with a perfect Niagara of words that left us almost breathless and ending finally in a voice that was scarcely audible. There is power in oratory, and nature never lavished this gift more freely than she did on B. H. Roberts.[14]

Another added, "When repelling an attack launched against his faith or his people he wields the rapier of defense 'as though the strength of twenty men were in his arm.' He is truly a formidable champion."[15]

When the church's politics-oriented Peoples Party was dissolved in 1891, and Mormons were asked to align themselves with one of the national political parties, Roberts and LDS Apostle Moses Thatcher (1842–1909) became Democrats.[16] Like Roberts, Thatcher was a graduate of the University of Deseret, a persuasive orator, and an ardent churchman who had been an apostle since 1879. He was described as a person who "combined in nice proportion the qualities of the dreamer and the fighter, the artist and the

---

14. Qtd. in Van Wagoner and Walker, *A Book of Mormons,* 245.

15. T. Pauly, "Brigham H. Roberts—A Tribute," *Improvement Era* 36 (November 1933): 783.

16. Thatcher was born in Sangamon County, Illinois, migrated with his family to the Great Salt Lake Valley in 1847, and went with them to California in 1849. The family moved to Logan, Cache Valley, in 1860, when Thatcher was eighteen. Always active in both church and business, Thatcher was a merchant, served as superintendent of Cache Valley schools, and was director and secretary of the Utah Northern Railroad Company. He later became vice president and director of ZCMI and Deseret National Bank and president of Thatcher Brothers Banking Company. After two years as Cache Valley Stake president, he was ordained an LDS apostle in 1879, was an active missionary and church diplomat, especially in Mexico, and was active in the colonization of Star Valley, Wyoming; San Luis County, Colorado; and northern Mexico. A counselor to the president of the Young Men's MIA, he published many articles in their magazine, *The Contributor.* Brief biographies of Thatcher are found in Whitney, *History of Utah,* 4:264–68; Jenson, *Biographical Encyclopedia,* 1:127–36; and Noble Warrum, *History of Utah Since Statehood,* 4 vols. (Chicago: S. J. Clarke Publishing Co., 1919–20), 4:5–7. See also Edward Leo Lyman, "The Alienation of an Apostle from His Quorum: The Moses Thatcher Case," in John Sillito and Susan Staker, eds., *Mormon Mavericks: Essays on Dissenters* (Salt Lake City: Signature Books, 2002), 159–92.

banker, the philosopher and the man of affairs."[17] In 1895, Roberts
and Thatcher were nominated by their party to the House of Representatives and US Senate. At the heat of the campaign, Joseph F.
Smith, a member of the First Presidency and staunch Republican,
declared in one of the church's general priesthood meetings that the
two men were out of harmony with "The Brethren" because they
had not cleared their political activities in advance. When Utah
statehood was imminent in the early 1890s, the general authorities had decided that "brethren holding prominent positions in
the church" should not become candidates for public office. This
was modified to permit "brethren" to accept nomination to the
constitutional convention, and high church officials, stake presidents, bishops, and patriarchs were thus elected and served. In fact,
the president of the convention, John Henry Smith (1848–1911),
was an apostle. At the close of the convention, when men were
nominated for state office, Roberts and Thatcher assumed church
rules permitted their acceptance. Believing that Joseph F. Smith's
statement was politically motivated, Roberts and Thatcher alleged
"ecclesiastical interference," and continued to campaign. Both were
narrowly defeated. Although both men "made acknowledgement"
to the First Presidency, both believed the intense Republican prefer-
ence of the First Presidency was a factor in their defeat.[18]

The First Presidency and Twelve Apostles then prepared a "Political

---

17. Warrum, *History of Utah Since Statehood,* 4:7.

18. The Roberts/Thatcher cases are discussed in Madsen, *Defender of the Faith,*
221–30; Edward Leo Lyman, *Political Deliverance: The Mormon Quest for Utah State-
hood* (Urbana: University of Illinois Press, 1986), 169–71, 268–76; B. H. Roberts,
Comprehensive History of the Church of Jesus Christ of Latter-day Saints, 6 vols. (Salt
Lake City: Deseret Book Co., 1930), 6:330–36; Calvin Reasoner, *Church and State:
The Issue of Civil and Religious Liberty in Utah* (Salt Lake City: Juvenile Instructor
Press, 1896); *The Thatcher Episode: A Concise Statement of the Facts in the Case* (Salt
Lake City: Deseret News Publishing Co., 1896); Stanley S. Ivins, *The Moses Thatcher
Case* (Salt Lake City: Modern Microfilm, n.d.); and N. L. Nelson, *An Open Letter to
Hon. Moses Thatcher* (Salt Lake City: Deseret News Publishing Co., 1897).

Manifesto" to stipulate that a general authority must secure approval before engaging in a campaign that might require duties inconsistent with his ecclesiastical office. Roberts and Thatcher objected and refused to sign. Both men were suspended from their ecclesiastical offices while "The Brethren" labored with them. They faced the dilemma of sacrificing principles or being stripped of their church blessings. Thatcher desired "to be one with [his] brethren" in religious matters but insisted on his independence in political matters. He could not sign the Political Manifesto, as worded, without personal "stultification."[19]

The Quorum of Twelve Apostles was divided, creating what was one of the bitterest political controversies in Utah history. Quorum President Lorenzo Snow said it reminded him of the "terrible spirit" in 1838–39 when there was dissension and apostasy in Kirtland, Ohio (see Chap. 1).[20] Shortly before the deadline, Roberts changed his mind and signed; Thatcher, caught up in the inner turmoil of a man trying to walk a tightrope between devotion to church and devotion to conscience, refused.[21] Roberts later explained that he had finally become convinced that Thatcher and he had humiliated "The Brethren" by charging them with political favoritism. Having signed the document, Roberts declared:

> I learned that it was my duty to yield completely to God's authority on earth and it was not for me to set up my judgment against the combined and united judgment of His servants. ... I was obedient, thank the Lord, to the promptings of the voice of that Spirit [the Spirit of the Lord]. I did not reject its instructions as I did those of the brethren; and though following its instructions cost the good opinion

---

19. Thatcher, Letter to Lorenzo Snow, April 6, 1896, in Reasoner, *Church and State.*

20. Lyman, *Political Deliverance,* 273.

21. Maxwell A. Miller, "Thatcher Resilenced," *Dialogue: A Journal of Mormon Thought* 19 (Summer 1986): 7.

and friendship [in outside circles] I prized; and though it has cost me to sacrifice many worldly ambitions and put a period to my political aspiration, there has not been a day that I have regretted my obedience to the voice of God's Spirit and my reconciliation to His servants.[22]

In the next election, with the approval of now-Church President Lorenzo Snow, Roberts again ran for the House and was elected, but the House refused to seat him because he was a practicing polygamist.[23] Thatcher remained an outstanding advocate of separation of church and state and was disfellowshipped on November 19, 1896. The "Thatcher Case" remained on people's minds for many years; but for Roberts, the episode ended.

During World War I, at age sixty, Roberts volunteered for service as a chaplain with the 145th Field Artillery in France.

During most of his adult life, Roberts published extensively: *The Gospel* (1888); *Life of John Taylor* (1892); *Outlines of Ecclesiastical History* (1893); *A New Witness for God* (1895); *The Missouri Persecutions* (1900); *The Rise and Fall of Nauvoo* (1900); *Mormon Doctrine of Deity* (1903); *Defense of the Faith and the Saints* (2 vols., 1907 and 1912); *The Atonement* (1911); *Divine Imminence and the Holy Ghost* (1912); and *The Mormon Battalion* (1916). He also edited the seven-volume *History of the Church* (beginning 1902) and wrote the six-volume *Comprehensive History of the Church* (1930).

After his graduation from the University of Deseret, Roberts became a voracious reader, devouring considerable quantities of history, science, philosophy, and religion. Few other LDS general leaders before or since have mastered such a range of scholarly works. Roberts's belief in the divine origins of Mormonism was

---

22. Roberts, Letter to Thatcher, November 6, 1896, LDS Family History Library, qtd. in Madsen, *Defender of the Faith*, 228–29.

23. Davis Bitton, "The Exclusion of B. H. Roberts from Congress," in Bitton, *The Ritualization of Mormon History and Other Essays* (Urbana: University of Illinois Press, 1994), 150–70.

unquestioned, but he often took a broader view of its place in the heavenly scheme of things than did some of his colleagues. In 1902, Roberts told the Saints that "while the Church of Jesus Christ of Latter-day Saints is given a prominent part in this great drama of the last days, it is not the only force nor the only means that the Lord has employed to bring to pass those things of which His prophets in ancient times have testified."[24] In the scientific and artistic advance of civilization, Roberts saw the hand of God. Mormonism, he said, is "one of the great world-movements for the accomplishment of the mighty purposes of God. It is connected with all the other great world movements that are bringing to pass the revolutions now going on in the earth." Through science, "physical conditions are being brought into existence that will coordinate with those spiritual and moral conditions which 'Mormonism' will yet establish and will bring to pass, the realization of the world's hope for that reign of peace and righteousness called the millennium." Roberts was anxious for all Saints to take advantage of educational opportunities to advance the cause of God.[25]

Roberts, an independent thinker who believed in human reason aided by divine revelation, left an indelible mark on the scholarly tradition of the church with his famous manual series, *The Seventy's Course in Theology*, in which he wrote in the last volume:

It requires striving—intellectual, and spiritual—to comprehend the things of God—even the revealed things of God. ... "Simple faith"—which is so often ignorant and simpering acquiescence, and not faith at all—but simple faith taken at its highest value, which is faith without understanding of the thing believed, is not equal to intelligent faith, the faith that is the gift of God, supplemented by earnest endeavor to find through prayerful thought and research a

---

24. Sermon of April 2, 1902, *LDS Conference Report, April 1902* (Salt Lake City: Church of Jesus Christ of Latter-day Saints, 1902), 14–16.

25. Ibid.

rational ground for faith—for acceptance of truth; and hence the duty of striving for a rational faith in which the intellect as well as the heart—the feeling—has a place and is a factor. … Whatever position other churches and their religious teachers may take, the Church of Jesus Christ in the New Dispensation can do no other than to stand for mental activity, and earnest effort to come to a knowledge of truth up to the very limit of man's capacity to find it.[26]

Although Roberts authored numerous doctrinal and historical works, as mentioned earlier, his magnum opus, "The Truth, The Way, The Life," the theological equivalent of his *Comprehensive History,* remained unpublished until 1994, when two editions were issued (Signature Books and *BYU Studies*). Both editions carry introductory essays by noted scholars and in both volumes Roberts's text is accompanied by notes of clarification and explanation.

Roberts's intention in "The Truth, The Way, The Life" was very ambitious: "a search for *The Truth*, as it relates to the Universe and to man; a consideration of *The Way* as it relates to the attainment of those ends which may be learned as to the purpose of man's earth-existence; and the contemplation of *The Life*—that will result from the knowledge of the Truth and the Way." The title was chosen, as biographer Truman G. Madsen observed, "because through a lifetime of reflection he saw that the great system of 'truth' that 'gives unity to all history and proper relationship to all existing; that fills life with a real meaning, and makes existence desirable,' centers in and is embodied in Jesus the Christ."[27]

Roberts's theology was bold and audacious, for it "combined elements of traditional fundamentalism with the modern liberal

---

26. Roberts, *The Seventy's Course in Theology, Fifth Year: Divine Immanence and the Holy Ghost* (Salt Lake City: Deseret News, 1912), 4, 5, 6.

27. Madsen, "The Meaning of Christ—The Truth, The Way, The Life: An Analysis of B. H. Roberts' Unpublished Masterwork," *BYU Studies* 15 (Spring 1975): 259–92.

doctrine of man and the optimism of the nineteenth century, and it required a bold, rebellious, and spacious mind to grasp its full implication." Roberts "not only shaped the outlines of a systematic theology but developed, as well, the perspectives which placed the Church as an institution within the framework of history and provided the Mormon people with the instrument of rationalizing and defending their beliefs and practices."[28]

Self-education, however rigorous and comprehensive, carries inevitable limitations. In nearly every discipline, Roberts, though possessing one of the finer minds Mormonism has produced, showed himself a wide-ranging explorer rather than a resident at home in his field. Without the benefit of association with other scholars, Roberts on occasion failed to discriminate between original thinkers and their popular imitators, between faddish trends and enduring movements.

Roberts's approach was bold and creative, but none of his doctrinal books became standard reference works as did two by Talmage. In addition to *Articles of Faith*, Talmage's *Jesus the Christ* (1915) is found in nearly every LDS home. *Jesus the Christ* is a blend of LDS scripture and conservative biblical scholarship. Whereas Roberts's approach was often to consider alternate points of view before settling on an LDS position, Talmage was concerned primarily to present LDS doctrine with careful precision, buttressed by evidence and argument from non-LDS sources when available. Talmage contributed importantly to the mainstream of LDS thought; Roberts introduced the Saints to some of the most advanced thinkers of the age. Both men died in 1933.

---

28. B. H. Roberts, *Joseph Smith the Prophet-Teacher*, with an introduction by Sterling M. McMurrin (Princeton: Deseret Club of Princeton University, 1967), introduction unpaged. Although Roberts was not in any sense a scientist, as a writer and exponent of science, he had an important impact on Mormon thought. See Erich Robert Paul, *Science, Religion, and Mormon Cosmology* (Urbana: University of Illinois Press, 1992).

W. H. Chamberlin

The spirit of learning and intellectual tolerance fostered by B. H. Roberts in his prominent church position was furthered by several LDS educators of the early twentieth century, foremost of whom was William H. Chamberlin (1870–1921).[29]

Personally, Roberts and Chamberlin were quite different. Roberts was outspoken, obstinate, ready to interject himself into the fray. Chamberlin was quiet and unassuming. Both men had an insatiable appetite for knowledge, but Roberts was largely self-educated. Chamberlin graduated from the University of Utah (1896), served a three-year LDS proselytizing mission to Tahiti, studied ancient languages and higher criticism at the University of Chicago (summers of 1901 and 1902), completed an MA degree in philosophy from the University of California, Berkeley, under George Howison (1906), studied psychology at the University of Chicago (summer 1907), and studied philosophy under Josiah Royce at Harvard (1907–08).

Though he published little, Chamberlin's contribution to the life of the mind in Mormonism was, like Roberts's, significant. Chamberlin's primary influence was in the classroom, where he taught many persons who later served as professors, department heads, and deans in universities attended by LDS students. He taught in public schools (1889–91); science and mathematics at the LDS College (1891–97); geology and mathematics, then theology at Brigham Young College (1900–01, 1903–04); philosophy and ancient languages at Brigham Young University (1909–16); and philosophy at the University of Utah (1917–20) and the Utah State Agricultural

---

29. Ralph V. Chamberlin, *Life and Philosophy of William H. Chamberlin* (Salt Lake City: Deseret News Press, 1925); Ephraim E. Ericksen, "William H. Chamberlin: Pioneer Mormon Philosopher," *Western Humanities Review* 8 (Autumn 1954): 277–85; and James M. McLachlan, "W. H. Chamberlin and the Quest for a Mormon Theology," *Dialogue: A Journal of Mormon Thought* 29 (Winter 1996): 151–67.

W. H. Chamberlin

College (1920–21). (Chamberlin's competence in so many fields is a reflection of *fin de siècle* Utah education.) Fourteen years younger than Roberts, Chamberlin died twelve years earlier, at age fifty.

When Chamberlin went to BYU in 1909, he joined brother Ralph (1879–1967) and Henry and Joseph Peterson (1868–1957; 1874–1943) on the faculty. Ralph had completed his PhD in biology at Cornell in 1905, the year the Peterson brothers graduated from the University of Chicago. Henry Peterson went on to a master's in psychology at Harvard (1906), and Joseph to a PhD in literature from Chicago (1907). BYU had recently been confirmed as the church university (over LDS University in Salt Lake City and Brigham Young College in Logan), and the four new faculty members hoped to help lift the quality of education at the school to the level of a major university. The four worked energetically to stimulate interest in intellectual pursuits. They spoke to church groups and student audiences on higher biblical criticism and evolution, and both subjects became popular topics for discussion on campus. Though other Latter-day Saints had advocated evolution as God's means of creation before the Chamberlins and the Petersons, none had attracted so much attention.[30]

Ralph Chamberlin spoke at a memorial service commemorating in 1909 the births of Charles Darwin and Abraham Lincoln, and described Darwin as one of the greatest scientific minds of the age. In the BYU student newspaper, he published "The Early Hebrew Conception of the Universe," and "Early Hebrew Legends," drawing upon higher criticism to point out the "constant evolution" of Hebraic thought and "the progressive unfolding of the divine Will" revealed in the Bible.

W. H. Chamberlin published an essay titled "The Theory of Evolution as an Aid to Faith in God and Belief in the Resurrection," in which the philosophy of "personal idealism" played an important role. Stressing divine immanence in the processes of nature, Chamberlin found in the theory of evolution evidence for faith in the Resurrection. He also spoke of the parabolic and mythical elements of the Old Testament, which when properly understood as literary and didactic elements disarmed critics of the Bible who objected to stories such as Jonah and the whale. In addition to accepting evolution and higher criticism, Joseph Peterson's theory of cognition challenged what some understood to be the LDS concept of free will.

Though the modernist ideas of the Chamberlins and the Petersons seem to have met with the approval of many faculty and students, Superintendent of LDS Education Horace H. Cummings

---

30. The 1911 BYU controversy is discussed in Duane E. Jeffery, "Seers, Savants, and Evolution: The Uncomfortable Interface," *Dialogue: A Journal of Mormon Thought* 8 (Autumn/Winter, 1973): 41–75; and in Gary James Bergera, "The 1911 Evolution Controversy at Brigham Young University," in Gene A. Sessions and Craig J. Oberg, eds., *The Search for Harmony: Essays on Science and Mormonism* (Salt Lake City: Signature Books, 1993), 23–41.

reported that more than a dozen LDS stake presidents had complained of heresies being taught at BYU by the new faculty members. Opposed to both higher criticism and evolution, Cummings was motivated by concern for the spiritual and religious welfare of the students. After a brief investigation, he asserted the teachers were "applying the evolutionary theory and other philosophical hypotheses to principles of the gospel and to the teachings of the Church in such a way as to disturb, if not destroy, the faith of the pupils."[31] The Petersons and Ralph Chamberlin were named as chief offenders. The Church Board of Education informed the three they would have to alter their teachings or face dismissal.

A storm of controversy was raised in the Salt Lake City and Provo press, heightened by the publication of a petition reportedly signed by 90 percent of the BYU student body protesting the board's action. Nevertheless, the decision remained, and the Petersons and Ralph Chamberlin left the university for teaching careers outside the church education system. William Chamberlin remained at BYU five more years, prepared his lectures with care, and enjoyed teaching among his people.[32]

Mormonism had had its first brush with modernism. In a sense, it was mild and successfully contained. There were no books banned, no excommunications or schisms.[33] No official church position was taken with regard to evolution or higher criticism. In

---

31. Qtd. in Wilkinson, *Brigham Young University*, 1:419.

32. Although attendance at Chamberlin's BYU religion and philosophy classes remained high, the administration denied permission to teach any religion classes in 1913, his name and courses were omitted from the 1914–15 catalogue, and in 1916 he was informed that he was being transferred to the department of education. Chamberlin resigned, spent a year of study at Harvard, then taught philosophy through the University of Utah Extension (1917–20) and Utah State University Extension (1920–21). Chamberlin, *Life and Philosophy*, 209, 211, 270.

33. For a review of the modernist-fundamentalist controversy, see Sydney Ahlstrom, *A Religious History of the American People* (New Haven, Connecticut: Yale University Press, 1972), 763–824, 839–41, plus bibliography.

a church magazine, *Juvenile Instructor*, President Joseph F. Smith wrote that the decision had only been not to discuss evolution in church schools. He described it as "a question of propriety [without] undertaking to say how much of evolution is true and how much false."[34]

By deciding not to decide the evolution question, Smith avoided a head-on confrontation between the newly educated Saints who found in it support for LDS doctrine and those of more traditional persuasion who perceived the seeds of apostasy. By removing such controversial issues from the classroom, LDS authorities hoped to avert a doctrinal crisis. The popularity of the professors' interpretations risked undermining the authority of the apostles and prophets as sole adjudicators of church doctrine.[35]

In the action against the professors, the prerogatives of the priesthood were affirmed, but not without repercussions. BYU gained an anti-intellectual reputation which persisted for the ensuing decade. To many Saints, much of the academic world became suspect; professions in the life sciences, religious studies, and philosophy were dubious.[36]

Several years before, Joseph F. Smith had cautioned about the

---

34. Smith, "Philosophy and the Church Schools," *Juvenile Instructor* 46 (April 1911): 209.

35. The institutionalization of prophecy has been a key factor in the strength and unity of Mormonism. Antinomian tendencies in Joseph Smith's day were minimized by allowing that every member was entitled to revelation, but only pertaining to his or her own sphere of responsibility. Only the president of the church is authorized to receive revelation or to declare doctrine for the entire church.

36. See Davis Bitton, "Anti-intellectualism in Mormon History," *Dialogue: A Journal of Mormon Thought* 1 (Autumn 1966): 111–34, with an accompanying reply by James B. Allen (134–40). Shortly after the BYU affair, E. E. Ericksen, a PhD student in philosophy at the University of Chicago, was visited by Superintendent Cummings and told that "the philosophy I was being taught at the University of Chicago was not the kind that was wanted by my Church," and "that should I be given a position in the church school system I would be in for trouble as were the BYU professors." Ericksen transferred to economics, but later passed his exams in both philosophy and economics. See Scott G. Kenney, ed., *Memories and Reflections: The Autobiography of E. E. Ericksen* (Salt Lake City: Signature Books, 1987).

possible dangers inherent in an education which focused exclusively on the importance of book-learning. In 1903, he admonished the Saints not to "allow our sons to grow up with the idea that there is nothing honorable in labor, except in be in the professions of law, or in some other light, practically unproductive ... employment. ... We need manual training schools instead of so much book-learning and the stuffing of fairy tales and fables, which are contained in many of our school books of today."[37] Higher education was good—up to a point. People should develop their minds, but not to such an extent that they lose touch with the lessons of day-to-day life; not to such an extent that speculative theories and abstractions begin to come between their actual lives and the word of the Lord.

Successors: John A. Widtsoe, E. E. Ericksen, and Joseph F. Merrill

James E. Talmage's successor as moderate doctrinal spokesman with a scientific background was John A. Widtsoe. Having served as president of the Utah State Agricultural College (now Utah State University) and the University of Utah, Widtsoe was ordained an LDS apostle in 1921. Returning from six years presiding over the church's European missions, Widtsoe became the editor of the church's *Improvement Era* in 1935.[38] Three years later, he began a monthly column in the magazine entitled "Evidences and Reconciliations," which, continuing to his death in 1952, answered such questions as: How does God have constant knowledge of the whole universe? Was the Fall of Adam inevitable? Why are the Latter-day Saints called a covenant people? The

---

37. *LDS Conference Report, April 1903,* 3.

38. John A. Widtsoe, *In a Sunlit Land: The Autobiography of John A. Widtsoe* (Salt Lake City: Deseret Book Co., 1954). Especially helpful is Dale C. LeCheminant, "John A. Widtsoe: Rational Apologist" (PhD diss., University of Utah, 1977). See also Alan K. Parrish, *John A. Widtsoe: A Biography* (Salt Lake City: Deseret Book Co., 2003).

first column responded to the question, What is the attitude of the church toward science? "Every scientific discovery," Widtsoe wrote, "may be incorporated into the Gospel, and ... therefore, there can be no conflict between true religion and correct science. The Church teaches that the laws of nature are but the immutable laws of the Creator of the universe."[39] One must be careful that the facts are accurately observed and that the interpretation of fact is labeled as inference, and not confused with fact, but there is no inherent conflict between science and religion, he stated.

Through the *Improvement Era*, numerous books—*Joseph Smith as Scientist* (1908), *A Rational Theology* (1915), *Priesthood and Church Government* (1939), *An Understandable Religion* (1944), *In Search of Truth* (1930)—and many official study course manuals and articles, Widtsoe greatly influenced the common understanding of LDS doctrine. The titles of his column and books are indicative of his approach. He was a systematizer and simplifier who sought to reconcile the fundamentals of LDS doctrine with the modern world. "Rational" and "understandable" were favorite words in the Widtsoe lexicon. Rather than become engaged in acrimonious controversy, Widtsoe downplayed differences and emphasized similarities. His scientific background enabled him to allay the fears of those who considered science a threat to religion and those who suspected an anti-intellectual bias on the part of some church leaders. Viewing organic evolution as a theory which could be revised by new data, for instance, he maintained an openness to scientific advance without jeopardizing theological orthodoxy.[40]

LDS theology was a rational system of universal, fundamental

---

39. "Evidences and Reconciliations," *Improvement Era* 41 (October 1938): 586.

40. "How Old Is the Earth," *Improvement Era* 41 (December 1938): 713; also "How Did the Earth Come Into Being?" (February 1939), "What Is the Origin of Life on Earth?" (March 1939), and "To What Extent Should the Doctrine of Evolution Be Accepted?" (July 1939).

John A. Widtsoe

E. E. Ericksen

Joseph F. Merrill

truths; knowledge of truth was humankind's highest possession; and true secular (scientific) knowledge and true spiritual (religious) knowledge agree, for truth is one harmonious whole. Revelation and reason are the ways of learning truth. One must have complete freedom to pursue truth.[41]

By training and profession, the dean and chief critic of LDS social philosophy after W. H. Chamberlin was E. E. Ericksen. A son of

---

41. See LeCheminant, "John A. Widtsoe," passim. An excellent volume by a scholar competent in LDS intellectual history and the history of modern science is Paul, *Science, Religion, and Mormon Cosmology*. See also Sessions and Oberg, *The Search for Harmony.*

immigrant Danish farmers, Ericksen attended the Brigham Young College in Logan, where he studied psychology, philosophy, and biblical scholarship under Mosiah Hall and William H. Chamberlin. At the University of Chicago, he studied philosophy under James H. Tufts, George H. Mead, and Edward S. Ames. After four years as principal of the church's Murdock Academy (Beaver, Utah), Ericksen was hired to teach philosophy at the University of Utah (1915–43), where he became, in turn, professor, department head, and dean.

In 1922, the University of Chicago published Ericksen's doctoral dissertation, *The Psychological and Ethical Aspects of Mormon Group Life,* an analysis of three periods of "maladjustment" in LDS history: Mormons and gentiles (the Joseph Smith period); Mormons and Nature (territorial period); and New Thought and Old Institutions (early twentieth century). Ericksen admired Joseph Smith's sensitivity to the spiritual needs of his people, and he praised Brigham Young's pragmatic genius in conquering a hostile environment, but he was critical of those twentieth-century students and speakers who, he said, had failed to come to grips with the religious challenges of their age. Critical of the church's conservative posture in a progressive era, Ericksen concluded, "What Mormonism needs today is the vitalization of its institutions which need to be put into use rather than merely contemplated. ... When Mormonism finds more glory in working out new social ideals than in contemplating past achievements or the beauty of its own theological system, it will begin to feel its old-time strength."[42]

The year his short book was published, Ericksen was called to sit on the general board of the church institution most concerned with social programs, the Young Men's Mutual Improvement Association, where, with great energy, he served thirteen years. He was influential in the development of the church's recreation program,

42. Ericksen, *The Psychological and Ethical Aspects of Mormon Group Life* (Chicago: University of Chicago Press, 1922), 99. See also Kenney, *Memories and Reflections.*

as well as the course of instruction.[43] After Ericksen's release from the board in 1935, he continued to lecture and to decry the rise of what he called the priestly mentality at the expense of the prophetic.[44] But he remained loyal to his LDS heritage and optimistic for its future. "In both thought and attitude," wrote LDS philosopher Sterling McMurrin (1914–96) in the 1975 reprint of *Mormon Group Life*, Ericksen "was a religious liberal in the best sense of that term, not seeking the destruction of faith, belief, or worship, but demanding that the Church and its religion come to terms with reason, science, and the dictate of the moral conscience. His was the first ... generation of authentic Mormon liberals, and he was their foremost philosophical spokesman."[45]

While Ericksen and his colleagues had been formulating innovative social thought and action in the MIA, their counterparts in the Church Education System were introducing recent historical research and biblical scholarship into church seminaries and Institutes. Sidney B. Sperry (1895–1977) was the first Latter-day Saint to earn a PhD in a divinity school.[46] In 1925, he began studies in the Old Testament languages and literature at the Chicago Divinity School, completing a master's degree in 1926 with a thesis on "The Text of Isaiah in the Book of Mormon." The following year, he became director of the church's first Institute of Religion at the University

---

43. In the early 1930s, Ericksen and James E. Talmage's daughter, Elsie T. Brandley, wrote two MIA manuals on *Challenging Problems of the Twentieth Century,* presenting the view of non-LDS scholars and social scientists on the economic, political, social, and religious problems current in the years of the Great Depression. Though popular with the church's young adults, a few church officials regarded it as too secular.

44. "Priesthood and Philosophy," *Utah Academy of Arts, Sciences and Letters Proceedings* 34 (1957): 13–22.

45. "Introduction" to Ericksen, *The Psychological and Ethical Aspects of Mormon Group Life,* reprint (Salt Lake City, 1975), x.

46. Russel B. Swensen, "Mormons at the University of Chicago Divinity School," *Dialogue: A Journal of Mormon Thought* 7 (Summer 1972): 37–47.

of Idaho, and after one year joined the religion faculty at Brigham Young University. He later received the PhD degree from the University of Chicago and was professor of Old Testament languages and literature at BYU. Meanwhile, Heber C. Snell (1883–1974), a teacher of education and psychology at Snow College in Ephraim, Utah, began his Old Testament studies at Berkeley's Pacific School of Religion. He was a student of William H. Chamberlin and E. E. Ericksen, and was editor of the student paper at the time of the 1911 BYU controversy. In 1928, at the BYU summer session for LDS seminary teachers, Snell offered a course in Old Testament literature. Sperry followed the next year, inspiring several teachers to follow his steps to Chicago Divinity School.

Joseph F. Merrill, who had resigned as Dean of Mines and Engineering at the University of Utah in 1928 to become Commissioner of LDS Church Education, was a strong advocate of higher education for seminary and Institute teachers. At Sperry's suggestion, Merrill persuaded Church President Heber J. Grant to approve the invitation of New Testament scholar Edgar J. Goodspeed (1871–1962) and three other faculty members from Chicago Divinity School to conduct six-week courses in biblical scholarship at the 1930 summer session at BYU for seminary teachers. Merrill also arranged to pay Daryl Chase (1901–84), George S. Tanner (1897–1992), and Russel B. Swensen (1902–87), three LDS seminary teachers, half salary as they began their advanced education at Chicago in the fall. By the end of the decade, seven more students arrived, most of whom completed PhDs in biblical studies or church history and returned to teach in the LDS Church system.[47]

---

47. Sperry, who also studied at the American School of Oriental Research and the Hebrew University in Jerusalem, and taught at BYU from 1952 to 1970; Snell of Snow College; T. Edgar Lyon, who went into Institute work and became director of Nauvoo Restoration, Inc.; Chase, in Church Education in 1932, dean of students at Utah State University, and president of USU (1954–68); Tanner, director of University of Idaho Institute, then at the USU Institute and director of the

Not all in Zion were pleased with the liberal and increasingly intellectual spirit beginning to manifest itself in the seminary and Institute system. Some church authorities cautioned teachers that they must stick to the revealed gospel, using as sources and authorities the standard works of the church and words of the prophets. World War II and the church's concern over unauthorized teachings infiltrating its educational system deterred many Latter-day Saints from attending divinity schools (but not other graduate schools) for a number of years. Nevertheless, the Chicago Divinity School group of the 1930s continued in church service. Nearly all had long careers in church education, including Russel Swensen, who completed his degree in New Testament and taught many years at BYU. He authored three LDS Sunday School manuals: *The Synoptic Gospels* (1945), *The Gospel of John* (1946), and *New Testament: Acts and Epistles* (1947), which demonstrated a positive attitude toward modern biblical scholarship while remaining well within LDS doctrinal orthodoxy.

o o o

LDS thought, with its strong individualism, has been too rich and challenging to be frozen in time or to be compressed between the covers of a single book. Every year new books and lesson manuals appear, adding gradually to the linear feet on library shelves taken up by LDS doctrinal works. While in a certain sense Latter-day Saints are not, and may never be, in the forefront of theological dialogue with their fellow Christians, due to the different premises from which they proceed, including the absence of "academic" theological training of LDS general authorities, there continues to be in LDS thought the vital process which has always generated theology in

---

Hawaiian Temple Bureau of Information; Swensen, BYU professor and author of church articles and manuals; Vernon Larsen; Wesley P. Lloyd, dean of students, dean of Graduate School at BYU, and graduate dean of the US International University; and Anthony S. Cannon, Institute teacher, FBI agent, and professor of sociology at the University of Utah (1947–66).

historical religions: reconciling statements within the canon, and additional pronouncements by later prophets with respect to the canon and to modern conditions—what the Latter-day Saint calls "continuous revelation." There has been and continues to be at least some awareness of developments in scriptural scholarship and of developments in other traditions where parallels might prove illuminating. Each year thousands of young Saints continue pursuing graduate degrees—a few in theology or religious studies, more in history and the social sciences, still more in psychology, medicine, and the natural sciences. There is little or no effort to insulate them from the ideas around them. Rather, home and church reinforce the religious life. As in all religious groups, there are some losses to the faith, but the LDS Church has proved strong in retaining the interest, loyalty, and involvement of its young people, including its intellectuals. In the traditional centers of Utah, in university cities and towns across the United States, and increasingly in Europe, Latin America, and Asia, intelligent, educated Saints seek fulfillment and expression in their church meetings and assignments but also in private study groups, private correspondence, and private periodicals not under the same constraints as those published officially by the church.

Such a situation may not be encouraging to those who like their Mormons to fit a common, simple mold. This was never so. But generally the LDS Church has drawn from its own traditions in allowing multiple kinds of expression and some latitude of belief and behavior. Perhaps the most careful expression of this point of view was that given in 1958 to the students and faculty of Brigham Young University by Hugh B. Brown, later to become First Counselor to Church President David O. McKay:

> We are very grateful in the Church and in this great university that freedom, dignity, and integrity of the individual is Church doctrine as well as in democracy. Here we are free to think and express our opinions. Fear will not stifle thought, as in the case of

some areas which have not yet emerged from the dark ages. God himself refuses to trammel man's free agency even though its exercise sometimes teaches painful lessons. Both creative science and revealed religion find their fullest and truest expression in the climate of freedom. ...

I hope that you will develop *the questing spirit.* Be unafraid of new ideas for they are the stepping stones of progress. You will, of course, respect the opinions of others but be unafraid to dissent—if you are informed.

Now I have mentioned freedom to express your thoughts, but I caution you that your thoughts and expressions must meet competition in the market place of thought, and in that competition truth will emerge triumphant. Only error needs to fear freedom of expression. Seek truth in all fields and in that search you will need at least three virtues: courage, zest, and modesty. The ancients put that thought in the form of a prayer. They said, "From the cowardice that shrinks from new truth, from the laziness that is content with half truth, from the arrogance that thinks it has all the truth—oh God of truth deliver us."[48]

---

48. Hugh B. Brown, address at Brigham Young University, March 25, 1958, as printed in *Dialogue: A Journal of Mormon Thought* 2 (Spring 1967): 136; emphasis added.

CHAPTER 5

J. Reuben Clark Jr.

CONSERVATIVE PHILOSOPHER

After the deaths of B. H. Roberts and James E. Talmage in 1933, there was, for a period of time, no clear statement as to the role of LDS schools and what should or should not be taught there. A concise answer was finally provided in 1938 by J. Reuben Clark Jr., representing the First Presidency, in a major address delivered on August 8, 1938, to LDS seminary and Institute of Religion teachers assembled at Aspen Grove, near Provo, Utah. The text of the speech was immediately printed in the "Church Section" of the church's *Deseret News* under the heading "First Presidency Sets Standards for Church Educators." In the speech that was also reprinted in the *Improvement Era* and in a separate pamphlet, Clark declared three fundamental beliefs, or key church doctrines, that are indispensable to the LDS message: (1) the divine birth of Jesus Christ and his literal physical resurrection, (2) "the Father and the Son actually in truth and very deed appeared to the Prophet Joseph [Smith]," and (3) Smith's "successors, likewise called of God, have received revelations." Each of these propositions, Clark stated, "together with all things necessarily implied therein or flowing therefrom, must stand, unchanged, unmodified, without dilution, excuse, apology, or avoidance; they may not be explained away or submerged," for "any individual who does not accept the fulness of these doctrines ... is not a Latter-day Saint." "You are not to teach the philosophies of the world, ancient or modern, pagan or Christian," Clark told the teachers, "for this is the field of the public schools. Your sole field is the Gospel, and that is boundless in its own sphere." "You are to teach this Gospel using as your sources and authorities the Standard Works of the Church, and the words of those whom God has called to lead His people in these last days. You are not, whether high or low, to intrude your own peculiar philosophy."[1]

Clark, an intelligent sophisticate, was plainly stating that the church would not use its tithing funds to undermine the three basic pillars: Jesus Christ, Joseph Smith, and the later prophets.

The talk, which was later included in the course of study for Melchizedek Priesthood quorums of the church and was the foundation for instructions given to the Church Commissioner of Education and the president of Brigham Young University, initiated a modification in the policy of openness in intellectual inquiry and support of science that had marked the Roberts–Talmage–Widtsoe years described in chapter 4. John A. Widtsoe continued to write, of course, although with less confidence in "the liberal spirit" than he had expressed before his mission to Europe from 1930 to 1934. "The times" seemed to call for a retreat from the ebullience of the earlier years of the century. As for BYU, the sciences continued to be strong there, including geology, physics, chemistry, bacteriology, and biology. Even in religion, one did not study only the standard works and statements by church leaders. Lowell Bennion's *Introduction to the Gospel,* when it appeared, was the standard introductory textbook, and in other religion classes, LDS history, for example, a variety of sources was used.

The "higher criticism" of the Bible and the scholarly analysis of biblical scholars that many Institute of Religion teachers had incorporated in their teaching and writing, however, was no longer welcomed, and intellectual speculations and ruminations were

---

1. J. Reuben Clark, "Church Section," *Deseret News,* August 13, 1938; also *Improvement Era,* September 1938.

J. Reuben Clark

discouraged; the "simple gospel" was to be taught and believed by all who gave instruction under official LDS auspices.

Joshua Reuben Clark Jr. was born in a small rock house three miles north of Grantsville, Utah, on September 1, 1871, the oldest of ten children born to Joshua Reuben Clark and Mary Louisa Woolley Clark.[2] His father, Indiana-born, was a Union soldier in the Civil War who went to Montana to mine in the 1860s and was converted to the LDS Church during a brief sojourn in Salt Lake City. His mother was the seventh of eight children born to Edwin D. and Mary Wickersham

---

2. The best sources are David H. Yarn, *Young Reuben: The Early Life of J. Reuben Clark., Jr.* (Provo, Utah: Brigham Young University Press, 1973); Frank W. Fox, *J. Reuben Clark: The Public Years* (Provo, Utah: Brigham Young University Press/Deseret Book Co., 1980); and D. Michael Quinn, *J. Reuben Clark: The Church Years* (Provo: Brigham Young University Press, 1983), subsequently expanded and republished as Quinn, *Elder Statesman: A Biography of J. Reuben Clark* (Salt Lake City: Signature Books, 2002). The entire issue of *BYU Studies* 13 (Spring 1973) is devoted to "J. Reuben Clark, Jr.: Diplomat and Statesman."

Woolley. A Quaker before he joined the LDS Church in 1842, Edwin Woolley became the business manager of Brigham Young in early Utah and was bishop of the Salt Lake City Thirteenth Ward for twenty-eight years, including the year J. Reuben was born. Reared in a struggling farming family, young Clark, usually called Reuben, helped to herd cattle, cut wood for the winter, and tended the crops grown on an irrigated farm. In his youth, Clark was actively involved in Grantsville Ward activities—giving recitations and talks, acting in plays, attending meetings, and delivering Fast Day offerings to the poor and needy. Both parents were intelligent and sought to give Clark a good education, but he did not start school until he was ten. He was an avid reader and excelled in the local ward school. The highest grade of instruction in Grantsville was the eighth; eager to learn all he could, Clark re-enrolled for an additional two years of the eighth grade.

When he was nineteen, Clark registered in the better schools in Salt Lake City, beginning with the Latter-day Saints College and then the University of Utah. To pay his expenses, he worked at the Deseret Museum as an assistant to James E. Talmage, curator-founder of the museum and president of the Latter-day Saints College. When Talmage became president of the University of Utah in 1894, he took along Clark as his assistant. Clark graduated from the University with a BS degree in science in 1898. Intensely political, he was president of the student body and editor of the student newspaper, *The Chronicle.* His valedictory address was enthusiastic about the Spanish–American War. Talmage said that Clark was the brightest student he had ever had.

The same year Clark graduated, he married Luacine Savage (1871–1944), daughter of Charles R. Savage, one of the West's finest photographers, in a ceremony performed by Talmage. For five years, Clark taught school in Utah, the first as a principal in Heber City; then as an instructor of English, Latin, and government at the LDS College in Salt Lake City; the third year at the State Normal

School in Cedar City, Utah; and the fourth and fifth years as teacher of typing and shorthand at the LDS Business College (successor to the Latter-day Saints College) in Salt Lake City.

In 1903, when he was thirty-two, the Clarks decided Reuben should go to law school and specialize in mining law. A teacher-friend at Latter-day Saints College, Joseph E. Nelson, advanced enough money for the Clarks and their two daughters to live a frugal lifestyle in New York City from 1903 until Reuben received a law degree from Columbia University in 1906. A brilliant student, Clark was elected during his second year to the board of the *Columbia Law Review* and admitted to the New York bar. He also helped distinguished professor James Brown Scott compile materials for a book on equity jurisdiction. The summer following Clark's graduation, Scott was appointed Solicitor of the State Department by US President Theodore Roosevelt. Scott appointed Clark Assistant Solicitor, to specialize in international law. Clark also taught classes at George Washington University Law School in Washington, DC. In three years, Clark had repaid Joseph Nelson's loan.

In 1910, Clark was appointed head solicitor of the Department of State, prepared memoranda for several important cases, served as a member of the board of the American Red Cross, was a director of the American Peace Society, and was counsel for the Tribunal of Arbitration on an agreement between the United States and Great Britain. He retired from the solicitor position in 1913, when Woodrow Wilson assumed the US presidency, and opened law offices in Washington, DC, New York City, and later in Salt Lake City.

By appointment from several US presidents, Clark served on numerous commissions and in many important positions for the federal government. During World War I, he served as a major in the Judge Advocate General's Office of the US Army, where he demonstrated thoroughness and industry.

Desiring to return to Utah, the Clarks moved to Salt Lake City in 1923, where Reuben took active charge of his law firm but continued to be summoned repeatedly by the US government to serve with the Washington Naval Conference, United States Mexican Mixed Claims Commission, Conference for the Limitation of Armaments, Undersecretary of State, legal advisor to the US Ambassador to Mexico, Ambassador to Mexico, and president of the Foreign Bondholders Protective Council.

Clark was a person of formidable mental prowess and a prodigious worker. He is especially noted for the *Clark Memorandum on the Monroe Doctrine,* which foreshadowed the renunciation of US military intervention in Latin America in the 1930s. He conducted a personal crusade against US membership in the League of Nations and World Court, and made two unsuccessful attempts to secure the Utah Republican nomination to the US Senate.

In 1933, after three years' service as the US Ambassador to Mexico, Clark was called by LDS Church President Heber J. Grant as a counselor in the First Presidency. Clark was sixty-two. In many ways, the appointment was unprecedented, as Clark had never been an LDS ward bishop, stake president, or held any other responsible church position; nor was he called at that time as an apostle. He served in the First Presidency as a counselor to Presidents Heber J. Grant, George Albert Smith, and David O. McKay for the next twenty-eight years, a longer period than any other counselor had served, until his death in 1961 at the age of ninety.

As a member of the First Presidency, Clark was the first president of KSL Radio Station, vice president of ZCMI, and held offices in other church corporations. Although Clark quit the world of international affairs to help the church, he devoted part of his energies during the first four years to serving as president of the Foreign Bondholders Protective Council, an organization created for the purpose of salvaging something for American holders of the mounting number of foreign government bonds in default.

The era in which the Clarks lived in the East, first in New York City while attending Columbia University and then in Washington, DC, as a solicitor for the State Department, was one of anti-Mormon hostility. Sermons were delivered in some Protestant churches urging congregations to root out "the Mormon evil" from American society. New LDS plural marriages were being performed; Utah citizens had elected B. H. Roberts, an acknowledged polygamist, to Congress; Reed Smoot, an LDS apostle, had been elected to the US Senate; scores of vicious articles appeared in national magazines, and some explicitly anti-Mormon books were in wide circulation. Clark found it necessary to make a choice: admit to his Mormonism or remain silent. Although he decided to acknowledge his culture, he remained for a time somewhat aloof from the church. At Columbia, he was preoccupied with his studies; in Washington, DC, he was advised by his superiors that, in order to be effective, he must play down his religion. A hard worker, often putting in fourteen-hour work days and frequently away from home on assignments, he did not attend church services regularly; he continued to study his faith but did not hesitate to raise questions about some doctrines and practices.

"Mormon" meetings in Washington were held in the home of Senator Smoot, and Clark did not like the senator's cold, austere manner. He found fault with the church's missionary program, and with the wearing of temple garments in the insufferable heat and humidity of Washington. He took a relaxed attitude toward the Word of Wisdom, and he fell behind in his tithing. With a vigorous and discriminating intellect, he moved from his boyhood unalloyed faith to a more complex, rational, and thoughtful attitude. As a student at Columbia, he was taught that lawyers should not accept anything on faith. He wrote:

> The lawyer must consider motives, he must tear off the mask and lay bare the countenance, however hideous. The frightful skeleton

of truth must always be exposed. ... Every conclusion had to be [exposed] to the fiery ordeal of pitiless reason, bringing to all doctrines, all preachments, and even the very scriptures themselves a final conclusive test. What he can himself reason out according to his standards, he accepts unqualifiedly; whatever cannot stand his tests, he rejects as unfit.[3]

But Clark soon changed; he moved away from the position of doubter, as he continued to acknowledge his culture. When a friend closed a letter with "trusting you are still in the Church and the Church is losing nothing on that account," Clark replied in the words of boxer John L. Sullivan after ten bare-knuckled rounds with Jake Kilrain in New Orleans, "Slightly disfigured, but still in the ring."[4]

As time went on, Clark came to believe that life was empty without the church. His immersion in professional concerns left something lacking. The workaholic was not experiencing spiritual fulfillment. To the delight of Luacine, they moved to Salt Lake City in 1923 and he began gradually to disentangle himself from the worldly values, perceptions, and style that he had partially embraced. Whether or not this was a conversion experience in the classical sense, Clark's decision had far-reaching consequences. He began attending church meetings with Luacine and became active in church affairs. In June 1925, he was appointed to the general board of the Young Men's Mutual Improvement Association. The following year, he was appointed a member of the advisory editorial committee of *The Improvement Era*. He addressed missionaries about foreign residency procedures and lectured tourists on LDS beliefs. Most significant was his teaching a Sunday school class in the Twentieth Ward on the life of Jesus. The subject took possession of him; he put in long hours of research and preparation for each lesson. He began shifting his attention from proof and reason to theology and

3. Qtd. from a Clark Memorandum in Fox, *The Public Years,* 431.
4. Ibid., 411.

the scriptures. Eventually, these lessons, with additional material, were published in his book *Our Lord of the Gospels* (1947).

Embracing things spiritual, Clark came to repudiate the values that had tempted him for twenty years. He told one friend that he now believed all he could and took the rest on faith.[5] It was this faithful stalwart who was called in 1933 to join the First Presidency. Fearful that total commitment to intellectual inquiry might lead to agnosticism and then to atheism, he urged the primacy of faith. He was suspicious of what he interpreted as the smugness of "intellectuals." As a private person and as a member of the First Presidency, he sought a conservative balance between the imperatives of reason and revelation.[6]

Clark's 1938 address cited at the beginning of this chapter cautioned LDS teachers against rationalizing the things of the spirit—"finite mind and reason cannot comprehend nor explain infinite wisdom and ultimate truth."[7] "The church's youth," he said, "must be taught the two great principles of the Gospel: That Jesus is the Christ and that Joseph Smith was God's prophet." Seminary and Institute of Religion teachers must have a testimony of the truthfulness of these principles. "No teacher who does not have a real testimony of the truthfulness of the Gospel as revealed to and believed by the Latter-day Saints, and a testimony of the Sonship and Messiahship of Jesus, and of the divine mission of Joseph Smith—including in all its reality the First Vision—has any place in the Church school system."[8]

The talk, oft-repeated in meetings of LDS educators, emboldened members of the Division of Religion at BYU to oppose certain

---

5. Ibid., 445.

6. Quinn, *The Church Years,* 169.

7. Clark, "The Charted Course of the Church in Education," *Improvement Era* 41 (September 1938): 570.

8. Ibid., 571.

scientists, social scientists, and professionals in the humanities who seemed to intellectualize religion and place it, for purposes of discussion, within the framework of philosophical or historical analysis. No further thought was given to sending bright seminary or Institute teachers to the University of Chicago or to any other divinity school with "modern" (i.e., non-LDS) biblical studies. On the other hand, for most of the Clark years, all, or nearly all, BYU professors taught religion classes in addition to their particular specialties. And, except for religion classes, most subjects at BYU and other LDS colleges were taught much the same at other colleges and universities.

Clark later set up a committee to screen material used in Sunday school, priesthood, seminary and Institute of Religion lesson manuals to counter what he regarded as the longstanding infusion of liberal theology into church lesson manuals. In the instructions to the committee, he stated, "Worldly knowledge and speculation have their place; but they must yield to revealed truth." Material must be "so framed and written as affirmatively to breed faith and not raise doubts."[9] He would not go so far as to excommunicate people suspected of having disloyal and apostate attitudes; but all church educational institutions must provide their secular training within a religious atmosphere that gave priority to faith in what Clark understood as the simple, orthodox gospel of Christ. Teachers were, of course, free to use other sources helpful to them in presenting their lessons.

Early Christian writers, Clark knew, had sought to reconcile Greek philosophy with Christ's teachings, and thus had corrupted the early church. In his own day, secular scholars who attempted to reconcile the gospel with the "higher criticism" of the Bible were, in Clark's view, doing the same. Those engaged in analyzing the reliability of various ancient texts of the Bible, the literary style and

---

9. Quinn, *The Church Years,* 169.

historical context of the Bible, and the original transmission and construction of the biblical narratives were taking away the divinity of Jesus and lessening the sacredness of the King James version.[10] Later, Clark instructed all superintendents of LDS Sunday schools and editors of publications to eliminate "paganistic theories and tenets of the so-called 'higher criticism' from all classes and publications." Higher criticism, he declared, denied the divine origin of scripture, was a "sinister school of thought," represented "pettifogging scholarship," and was an "attack upon God and Christianity."[11] This was preliminary to his final statement on the matter, the 473-page *Why the King James Version?* (1956). To Clark, the King James Version "was not simply a Biblical translation, but it was *the* Bible [at least for English readers], and he used scholarly sources to defend that supremacy."[12]

Clark's view of modern scholarship and higher education in general was clearly expressed in his 1938 Aspen Grove talk:

> For any Latter-day Saint psychologist, chemist, physicist, geologist, archaeologist, or any other scientist, to explain away, or misinterpret, or evade or elude, or most of all, to repudiate or to deny, the great fundamental doctrines of the Church in which he professes to believe, is to give the lie to his intellect, to lose his self-respect, to bring sorrow to his friends, to break the hearts and bring shame to his parents, to besmirch the Church and its members, and to forfeit the respect and honor of those whom he has sought, by his course, to win as friends and helpers.[13]

---

10. Ibid., 174–75. Widtsoe had written in his 1930 book, *In Search of Truth,* that "Higher criticism is not feared by Latter-day Saints," and added, "To Latter-day Saints, there can be no objection to the careful and critical study of the scriptures, ancient or modern, provided only that it be an honest study—a search for truth" (*In Search of Truth* [Salt Lake City: Deseret Book Co., 1930], 81, 90).

11. Quinn, *The Church Years,* 176. See also Philip L. Barlow, *Mormons and the Bible* (New York: Oxford University Press, 1991), 158–81.

12. Quinn, *The Church Years,* 177.

13. Clark, "The Charted Course," 572.

In 1979, no doubt influenced by Clark's position, church authorities published an LDS edition of the King James Version, heavily cross-referenced with other LDS scriptures. It was almost as though updating the language of translation to contemporary standards threatened inspiration itself.[14]

If Clark was concerned to protect the spiritual welfare of the Latter-day Saints, he was equally concerned with their temporal welfare. He had been called to the First Presidency in 1933, the bottom year of the worst depression in US history. Many Saints were unemployed, families were starving, and were seeking public welfare help from the cities, counties, and states where they were living. The church had always had a minimal welfare program to care for the aged, disabled, sick, and those suffering from natural calamities. But the Great Depression offered problems that significantly magnified the previous experience.

Turning away from government relief and advocating enlarged church effort, in July 1933 Clark drafted a comprehensive 28-page pamphlet entitled "Suggestive Directions for Church Relief Activities." The pamphlet outlined what was basically a new church welfare plan, including many aspects of the final version of the program inaugurated in April 1936.[15]

During the months that followed, a church survey determined the number of people receiving government relief, the number receiving help from the church, the number unemployed, and the number of families continuing to suffer. The final plan, the product of long administrative deliberations by church leaders, was adopted April 7, 1936, and incorporated the following provisions.[16]

---

14. Barlow, *Mormons and the Bible,* 179.

15. Garth Mangum and Bruce Blumell, *The Mormons' War on Poverty: A History of LDS Welfare, 1830–1990* (Salt Lake City: University of Utah Press, 1993), 119.

16. Sources on the church's Welfare Program include Mangum and Blumell, *The Mormons' War on Poverty*; Albert E. Bowen, *The Church Welfare Plan* (Independence, Missouri: Zion's Printing and Publishing Company, 1946); "Taking Care of

1. Persons in need should depend first on help from the family, second on Church welfare, and only on government help if absolutely necessary.

2. The Church would finance the program from fast offerings, donations, and from tithing when other sources were inadequate.

3. Church officials would make every effort to find employment for those in need. For that purpose, ward, stake, and general Church employment officers and committees were appointed.

4. Each LDS stake should inaugurate a production enterprise—a farm to raise foodstuffs, a cannery, a tannery, a clothing manufacturing company, or other needed and practical enterprise. The General Welfare Committee would consult with local officials on the best enterprise for the overall good of the Church.

5. Each ward and/or stake should maintain a bishop's storehouse to store food and clothing to be distributed to the needy.

6. Deseret Industries, operated much as Goodwill Enterprises of California, were to receive clothing and other products and the unemployed were to work repairing, cleaning, and selling goods to prospective customers.

In announcing the plan, Clark said: "Whether we shall now take care of our own Church members in need and how fully, depends wholly and solely upon the faith and works of the individual Church

---

Their Own: The Mormon Welfare System, 1936–1975," in Leonard J. Arrington, Feramorz Y. Fox, and Dean L. May, *Building the City of God: Community and Cooperation Among the Mormons* (Salt Lake City: Deseret Book Co., 1976), 337–58; Leonard J. Arrington and Wayne K. Hinton, "Origin of the Welfare Plan of the Church of Jesus Christ of Latter-day Saints," *BYU Studies* 5 (Winter 1964): 67–85; George Stewart, Dilworth Walker, and E. Cecil McGavin, *Priesthood and Church Welfare: A Study Course for the Quorums of the Melchizedek Priesthood for the Year 1939* (Salt Lake City: Deseret Book Co., 1939); and many articles in *The Improvement Era*, 1936–69, and in *Ensign*, 1970–94; Quinn, *The Church Years*, 251–78; L. Brent Goates, *Harold B. Lee: Prophet & Seer* (Salt Lake City: Bookcraft, 1985), 138–54.

members. If each Church member meets fully his duty and grasps his full opportunity for blessing, full necessary relief will be extended to all needy Church members; insofar as individual members fail in their duty and opportunity, by that much will the relief fall short."[17]

The following October, he added: "Our primary purpose ... was to set up, in so far as it might be possible, a system under which the curse of idleness would be done away with, the evils of the dole abolished, and independence, industry, thrift and self respect be once more established amongst our people. The aim of the Church is to help the people to help themselves. Work is to be re-enthroned as the ruling principle of the lives of our Church membership."[18]

Much emphasis was placed on "getting off government relief." Clark chastised church members with cattle, hay, and chickens who had, nonetheless, accepted relief. Relief was not for those who did not need it: "The thought that we should get all we can from the government because everybody else is getting it, is unworthy of us as American citizens. It will debauch us. ... We must be as careful with the government's funds as with our own or as with the Church's."[19]

Within six weeks of the announcement, more than 200 welfare projects were established in the church's stakes, and by the end of 1936 more than 17,000 people had worked on the welfare projects.[20] Fast offerings had increased by 50 percent, and church expenditures for the needy had doubled. A massive Bishop's Central Storehouse complex was built at 700 West and 700 South in Salt Lake City, with others elsewhere.

Some Latter-day Saints began to think that the Welfare Plan was intended to reestablish the United Order, that idealistic reordering

---

17. Cited in Mangum and Blumell, *The Mormons' War on Poverty*, 132.

18. Ibid., 138.

19. Clark, Sermon in *LDS Conference Report, October 1933* (Salt Lake City: Church of Jesus Christ of Latter-day Saints, 1933), 102. See also Arrington and Hinton, "Origins of the Welfare Plan," 78–79.

20. Quinn, *The Church Years*, 265.

of economic affairs to achieve greater equality. Unsuccessful attempts to institute the program had been made by Joseph Smith in Missouri in the 1830s and by Brigham Young in the 1870s. Clark announced that the immediate intention was to remove the 68,000 needy Saints from government relief rolls and make them self-supporting. Relief, he said, was the responsibility of churches and charitable organizations, not a proper problem of government.[21] Many concluded that the program was politically motivated—"an ultra-conservative gesture of withdrawal."[22] By 1939, the church was providing assistance to 155,460 Latter-day Saints. In 1946, the program became international as the church sent 85 freight cars of food, clothing, and bedding to Saints in war-devastated Europe. By 1960, the assets of the Welfare Plan had increased from $4 million to $44 million. Clark's contribution to the welfare of the Saints has left a lasting legacy.[23]

Several other LDS practices were innovations advocated by Clark: establishment of regional priesthood leadership, closed-circuit media broadcasts of general conferences in outlying wards and stakes, simultaneous translation of general conferences into the non-English languages of listeners, and construction of multi-ward buildings. Although he resisted many social changes, and the intellectualization of doctrine, he was innovative in church administration.[24]

Clark also significantly impacted church finances by the establishment of a general church budget for each year's expenditures. Church leaders, he said, must protect the sacred trust of donated monies by the most careful expenditure of funds. Administration of church finances was reorganized, responsibilities for the receipt and disbursement of funds were clearly outlined. With respect to

---

21. Ibid., 268.
22. Ibid., 269.
23. Mangum and Blumell, *The Mormons' War on Poverty*, 278.
24. Ibid., 281.

the operation of church businesses, certain other principles were recommended: "We start out with the basic purpose and mission of the Church which may be briefly stated thus: To work out the purposes of God among and for His children upon this earth by saving the living and by saving the dead. Therefore, the test of every Church financial operation, both incoming and outgoing, is, Does this help to carry out the purpose and mission of the Church? This principle we have behind us at all times."[25] Church-owned businesses, Clark said, were "part of the sacred trust of the Church rather than the freewheeling enterprise of capitalism."[26]

Clark also challenged "the incessant adulation of prominent pioneer leaders of Mormonism rather than the common folk of pioneering, and the tendency of present Latter-day Saints to bask in the reflected glory of their ancestors."[27] He taught that each individual must stand on his or her own accomplishments before God, and that there is no place for an aristocracy in the church.

In 1947, Clark delivered a classic sermon in general conference, "To Them of the Last Wagon," a tribute to the rank and file among the early LDS pioneers. He acknowledged the leadership of Brigham Young and his associates, but his central message was, "The building of this empire was not done in a corner by a select few but by this vast multitude flowing in from many nations." These faithful ones "measured to their humble calling and to their destiny as fully as Brother Brigham and the others measured theirs."

Clark described the leaders of a typical pioneer wagon train as marching out in front, "where the air was clear and clean and where they had unbroken vision of the blue vault of heaven." But back in that symbolic last wagon, "the blue heaven was often shut out from their sight by heavy, dense clouds of dust. ... Sometimes

---

25. Quinn, *The Church Years,* 274.
26. Ibid., 275.
27. Ibid., 103.

they glimpsed, for an instant ... the glories of a celestial world but it seemed so far away, and the vision so quickly vanished" through their weariness and heartache. Yet, with all the trouble of sick oxen, broken axles, and the delays of caring for children, it was around that last wagon that the angels of God would gather, giving strength and comfort in times of illness or attending at the birth of a new baby.

In considering economic standing, social standing, church standing, or class standing, Clark would urge us to beware of making too much of the honors and ranks created by men. These temporary, often forgotten artificial statuses can confuse and mislead us. God knows why some of us linger in those last wagons. He knows why our prayers must take a little longer and why our wagons are a little weaker. Thus could Clark offer his respect to "these humble but great souls ... solid as the granite mountains from which they carved the rocks for their temple," and ask the Lord to help the rest of us meet our duties as well as they met theirs.[28]

Clark was a complex person with some paradoxical opinions. He was a dedicated conservative, but at the same time he was anti-militaristic, anti-imperialistic, espoused human rights, was hostile to big business, had respect for foreign values, and had sympathy for the underdog. He was consistent and solid; yet he reversed himself on support of world organization, on pacifism, on interventionism, and even on religion. He found joy and meaning in work, but prized his friendships, his children, his marriage, his Mormonism.[29] One of his biographers summarized: "He was the anchor of the Church, the genius behind its temporal affairs, the symbol of strength to which Mormons the world over could look and hold, the man who stood ever staunch, ever faithful, ever true."[30] He

---

28. Bruce C. Hafen, "J. Reuben Clark: The Man and the Message," *BYU Today* 42 (September 1988): 3.

29. Fox, *The Public Years*, 602–03.

30. Ibid., 606.

saw dangers in rationalized religion, but was not dogmatic about unessential issues. He opposed war but was strongly opposed to Communism. Because of the advanced age and physical disabilities of the presidents he served, he carried heavy administrative loads, but operated with restraint, taking no authority to himself. He once defined himself as follows:

> I am pro-Constitution, pro-Government, as it was established under the constitution, pro-free institutions, as they have been developed under and through the Constitution, pro-liberty, pro-freedom, pro-full and complete independence and sovereignty, pro-local government, and pro-everything else that has made us the free country we had grown to be in the first 130 years of our national existence.
>
> It necessarily follows that I am anti-internationalist, anti-interventionist, anti-meddlesome-busybodiness in our international affairs. In the domestic field, I am anti-socialist, anti-Communist, anti-Welfare State. I am what the kindlier ones of all these latter people with whom I am denying any association or sympathy, would call a rabid reactionary. (I am not, in fact, that.)[31]

To that list, one must add that Clark was a watchman on Zion's tower who raised a warning voice to the Saints about the dangers he perceived in religious and secular spheres.[32] If Clark had any weakness, it was that he had little sense of historical development. The church was a given, its organization completed, the quality of the institution unchanging. Clark's work was that of a gifted legal mind who saw the church in terms of what it had become, not what it had been. The middle years of the twentieth century—the last years of Clark's life—were years of growth in membership, expansion into new countries and new fields of thought, and a growing sophistication in LDS

---

31. J. Reuben Clark Jr., *Our Dwindling Sovereignty* (Salt Lake City: Deseret News Press, 1952), 4–5.

32. Quinn, *The Church Years,* 195.

scholarship and understanding. With Clark's death in 1961, a new leadership emerged to direct the church. In addition to President David O. McKay, whose administration continued to 1970, many of the new leaders were men trained by Clark, especially Harold B. Lee, Marion G. Romney, and Gordon B. Hinckley.

Despite a brilliance of mind and speech, Clark shrank from the complex and abstract and felt a lifelong estrangement from those whom he referred to as "so-called intellectuals."[33] No one who knew Clark, however, would have suggested that he denigrated reason. He joined other thoughtful Saints in giving support to the three contemporaries profiled in the next chapter who honestly confronted the conflicts between faith and reason and for whom ideas were entities that had a life of their own. Clark would have agreed with them that intellectual excellence is part of spiritual excellence.[34]

---

33. Ibid., 163.
34. Hafen, "J. Reuben Clark: The Man and the Message," 3.

CHAPTER 6

Lowell Bennion, Henry Eyring, and Hugh Nibley

FAITHFUL INTELLECTUALS

Lowell Bennion, Henry Eyring, and Hugh Nibley were exemplary Latter-day Saints of thought who believed that faith and intellect were compatible, that the religious and secular were intertwined, and that men and women can maintain integrity in both spheres of life. All three were scholars who were devoted to the LDS Church and its mission. Their teaching, speaking, and writing demonstrate the harmony that is possible when creative, trained intellects are placed in the service of religious faith.[1]

Lowell Bennion

A less forceful personality than J. Reuben Clark, more liberal in sentiment and intellectual values, Lowell Bennion was described

---

1. Another leading LDS intellectual was Sterling McMurrin (1914–96). I leave him out of this review of leaders of faith and intellect primarily because in 1960 he was released from teaching Sunday school because of his unorthodox beliefs. The other three men in this group—Bennion, Eyring, and Nibley—continued their church activity despite views that were regarded by some as non-traditional. McMurrin's publications included *The Philosophical Foundations of Mormon Theology* (Salt Lake City: University of Utah Press, 1959); *The Theological Foundations of the Mormon Religion* (Salt Lake City: University of Utah Press, 1965); and *Religion, Reason, and Truth—Historical Essays in the Philosophy of Religion* (Salt Lake City: University of Utah Press, 1982). See also Sterling M. McMurrin and L. Jackson Newell, *Matters of Conscience: Conversations with Sterling M. McMurrin on Philosophy, Education, and Religion* (Salt Lake City: Signature Books, 1996).

by many close associates as perhaps the most Christ-like person they had ever known.[2] Writer of dozens of manuals used in LDS classes, author of many books Latter-day Saints have read, teacher of a whole generation of youth, Bennion educated the heart, conscience, and mind of LDS members, and had an indelible influence on LDS intellectuals. His thirty books and study manuals and more than a hundred essays demonstrate broad competence in philosophy, religion, social and personal ethics, sociology, scripture, history, practical living, education, world religions, politics, and a range of specifically LDS topics.[3]

Bennion was born into a devout LDS family of eight children in Salt Lake City in 1908, the son of Milton S. and Cora Lindsay Bennion. During most of Bennion's youth, his father was dean of the School of Education and director of the Summer School of the University of Utah. Also active in LDS Church and civic work, Milton Bennion served for several years (1943–49) as general superintendent of the Sunday schools of the church and authored *Moral Teachings of the New Testament* (1928). Lowell said that his parents often invited distinguished philosophers, scholars, writers, and visiting professors to dinner, so that the children grew up with freedom of thought and breadth of ideas.[4]

In 1928, Bennion graduated from the University of Utah in history and political science, and then went to Germany as an LDS

2. Peggy Fletcher, "Saint for All Seasons: An Interview with Lowell L. Bennion," *Sunstone* 10 (February 1985): 7–17; and Douglas D. Alder, "Lowell L. Bennion: The Things That Matter Most," in Philip L. Barlow, ed., *Teachers Who Touch Lives* (Bountiful, Utah: Horizon Publishers, 1988), 13–28. For a book-length biography, see Mary Lythgoe Bradford, *Lowell L. Bennion: Teacher, Counselor, Humanitarian* (Salt Lake City: Dialogue Foundation, 1995).

3. A nearly complete bibliography is found in Eugene England, ed., *The Best of Lowell L. Bennion: Selected Writings 1928–1980* (Salt Lake City: Deseret Book Co., 1988), 287–95. See also Philip Barlow, *Mormons and the Bible* (New York: Oxford University Press, 1991), 194–205.

4. Fletcher, "Saint for All Seasons," 7.

Lowell Bennion

proselytizing missionary, just thirty days after marrying Merle Colton (1906–94). She joined him at the end of the mission so the two could live together as he pursued graduate studies in Europe. He studied first in Erlangen in Germany and the University of Vienna, but when Adolf Hitler came to power, he went to Strasbourg University in France, where he studied philosophy, economics, sociology, and religion and completed a dissertation on *Max Weber's Methodology* (Paris, 1933).

When the Bennions returned to Utah in January 1934, no jobs were available in universities, so he was employed as an educational advisor for the federally directed Civilian Conservation Corps (CCC). Late in the same year, John A. Widtsoe, LDS Church Commissioner of Education, asked him to open an Institute of Religion adjacent to the University of Utah. (Previous LDS Institutes had been in operation next to the University of Idaho in Moscow, Idaho State University in Pocatello, and Utah State University in

Logan.) The purpose of the Institute, as Widtsoe explained, was to help LDS college students keep the faith and give them training in religion equivalent to what they were learning in classes on campus. As Church Commissioner, Widtsoe reinforced the earlier influence of Bennion's father and the integration into the gospel of human scholarship and experience.

Throughout the rest of his life, Bennion used a coherent reasoned approach to give an understandable and personally moving explanation of the Atonement—of the way in which Jesus saves us from mortality, ignorance, and sin. As LDS essayist Eugene England pointed out, Bennion's writing was a major factor in giving LDS theology more elegant intellectual shape and in revealing its powerful moral implications. As articulated by Bennion, LDS theology provides "a marvelous affirmation of the eternal God-like nature of all humans and culminates in the call to respond to Christ's uniquely saving power and to serve Him in ways that fulfill our own and others' needs and nature."[5]

After two years at the Salt Lake Institute of Religion, Bennion was sent to Arizona to establish an LDS Institute at Tucson. After two years, 1937–39, he returned to the Salt Lake Institute and remained there until 1962. Meanwhile, at Widtsoe's request, Bennion wrote *What About Religion?* (1934), the MIA manual which several thousand young LDS men and women, myself included, studied in 1934–35. In 1940, Bennion wrote *The Religion of the Latter-day Saints*, which was used as the college text in LDS theology for the next fifteen years. In 1955, he revised the book into *An Introduction to the Gospel*, which was used as a standard LDS Sunday school manual until 1970. Still one of the best systematic versions of LDS theology, *An Introduction* demonstrates the coherent moral and spiritual force in LDS thought.

---

5. England, "Introduction: The Achievement of Lowell Bennion," in England, ed., *The Best of Lowell Bennion,* xxiii.

Bennion also wrote many articles for *The Improvement Era, LDS Millennial Star,* and *Week-day Religious Education,* the periodical of the LDS Church Education System, as well as other manuals for the Primary, Sunday School, Relief Society, and Young Men and Young Women on LDS doctrine, the Old Testament, the New Testament, courtship and marriage, the Book of Mormon, the prophets, practical religion, leadership, life of Jesus, forgiveness, repentance, faith and reason, and Christianity. These were the days when no LDS Correlation Committee screened manuals, and writers were allowed considerable freedom in how they organized and presented their creative work.

In 1948, Bennion's talk at the Joseph Smith Memorial Lecture at the LDS Institute in Logan was on the creative mind and generous spirit of the church's founding prophet. He stressed Joseph Smith's contribution to Christian thought that all humans have eternal god-like being in themselves and were not created from nothing. They have the possibility of eternal progression. Thus their natures require and yearn for expansion, love, and meaning beyond the earthly and material. "The truly religious person learns to thrill in the satisfaction that comes from freely living in harmony with God's laws."[6]

Bennion's most thoughtful work on intellectual life and religion was his book *Religion and the Pursuit of Truth,* published by LDS Church-owned Deseret Book in 1959. The book was written to help LDS university students of science and philosophy harmonize their newly won knowledge with the religious faith they acquired at home and in church and to help students accept both traditions as being valid and of infinite worth. A person of rigorous personal integrity and a defender of truth, Bennion was "a lifelong example of the best Mormonism can produce."[7]

Persuaded by statements of Jesus, Bennion was among those

---

6. England, *The Best of Lowell Bennion,* xxii.
7. Fletcher, "Saint for All Seasons," 1.

who prayed for a revelation granting the priesthood to persons of all races. (Since the mid-1800s, the church had prohibited black members from ordination to the priesthood and participation in most LDS temple ceremonies. The ban was lifted in 1978.) Some Church Education administrators, regarding such a revelation as premature, released him as director of the Salt Lake Institute in 1962. He was appointed associate dean of students and professor of sociology at the University of Utah, serving 1962 to 1972. For many years thereafter, he was director of the Community Services Council. He also served with the Salt Lake Association of Retarded Citizens, Salt Lake Commission on Youth, and the Human Resources Council. With an intuitive compassion for all people, he also owned and operated a Boys Ranch in Teton Valley, Idaho, for over twenty-five years.

Gentle in manner, Bennion loved the Hebrew prophets Amos, Hosea, Micah, Isaiah, and Jeremiah—their ethical monotheism, their emphasis on justice and mercy. He loved the Sermon on the Mount and the teachings of Jesus. Other favorites were Mosiah 18 and Alma 32, the Book of Job, and some of the Psalms. He saw revelation as a two-way communication between human beings and the divine. "Behold, I am God and have spoken it; these commandments are of me … and were given unto my servants in their weakness, after the manner of their language, that they might come to an understanding" (D&C 1:24–28).

"I fear," Bennion wrote, "that we emphasize the unique things of Mormonism. We should practice Christianity not just Churchianity." Bennion, who was proud to be termed a liberal, described the designation as follows: "A liberal is concerned with people and adapting the theology and the church structure to serve human values. And a liberal is open-minded, free to think even in matters religious."[8]

---

8. Ibid., 12.

Bennion's principal concerns were five: that we not equate the religious life with church activity; that we not allow institutional goals to become ends in themselves; that we not think that the ordinances of the church have value in and of themselves apart from the quality of our lives; that we not identify being LDS primarily with things peculiar and distinctive in our religion; and that as we take pride in materiality, we do not divert our efforts from more genuine religious goals. The church is a wonderful means of helping people to become true disciples of Christ.[9]

When a special surprise celebration was held for Bennion on the occasion of his eighty-fifth birthday, Marion D. Hanks, a president of the LDS Seventies who had taught in the Salt Lake Institute with Lowell, described him using words from the 78th Psalm: "So he fed them according to the integrity of his heart; and guided them by the skillfulness of his hand."

Lowell's wife, Merle, died in 1994. Lowell died not quite two years later, in 1996.

Henry Eyring

The LDS Church has had several world-renowned scientists, partly because of the church's teaching that all truths, whether scientific, philosophical, or religious, emanate from God, and the equally important belief that men and women have unlimited potential to be achieved by education and experience. These people of stature in the scientific community include James E. Talmage, John A. Widtsoe, mentioned in chapter 4, and Harvey Fletcher (1884–1981) and Franklin S. Harris (1884–1960). Perhaps the most distinguished and widely known Latter-day Saint scientist was Henry Eyring.

Eyring was born in 1901 in the LDS colony of Colonia Juarez,

---

9. Bennion, "Reflections on the Restoration," *Dialogue: A Journal of Mormon Thought* 18 (Fall 1985): 160–67. See also Bennion, "The Uses of the Mind in Religion," *BYU Studies* 14 (Autumn 1973): 47–55.

Henry Eyring

Mexico, the third child and first son in a rather well-to-do ranching family that consisted of eighteen children. His father, Edward Christian Eyring, and mother, Caroline Cottam Romney, gave him important responsibilities as a child; he loved working and riding on the ranch. When he was eleven, the colonists left Mexico, and the Eyrings settled in Pima, a village on the Gila River in southeastern Arizona. In this community, he completed grade school, tried his hand at mining, and was awarded a $500 scholarship to attend the University of Arizona. When Eyring was preparing to leave for college, his father took him aside and said,

> Henry we've ridden together on the range, and we've farmed together. I think we understand each other. ... In this Church you don't have to believe anything that isn't true. You go over to the University of Arizona and learn everything you can, whatever is true is a part of the gospel. The Lord is actually running this universe. I'm convinced that he inspired the Prophet Joseph Smith. ... If you'll

live in such a way that you'll feel comfortable in the company of good people, and if you go to church and do the other things that we've always done, and if you seek the truth, then I don't worry about your getting away from the Lord.[10]

Eyring earned a bachelor's degree in mining engineering in 1922, then went to work in a copper mine. When a rock smashed his foot, he left the mine and enrolled for a master's degree in metallurgy. The noxious fumes of the blast furnaces induced him to pursue another field, and he returned for a PhD to become a teacher. He earned a doctorate in chemistry in 1927 at the University of California at Berkeley and stayed on as a professor for a brief period. Transferring to the University of Wisconsin, he met Mildred Bennion (1896–1969), chair of women's physical education at the University of Utah, in Wisconsin for a temporary visit. They married in 1928.

At Wisconsin, Eyring became interested in reaction kinetics. After a year of special study at Berlin and another at Berkeley, he wrote a paper creating an absolute rate theory, with imaginative applications to chemical and physical processes. The theory became an indispensable tool in the study of rates in chemical reaction, with applications not only in chemistry, but also in biology, engineering, geology, and physics. For this and other contributions, Eyring received the National Medal of Science, the highest honor bestowed on a scientist by the president of the United States; the $100,000 Wolf Prize in Chemistry, second only to the Nobel Prize; the Joseph Priestley Celebration Award, from the American Chemical Society; and the Berzelius Gold Medal from the Swedish Academy of Sciences.

The research also prompted an invitation in 1931 for Eyring to join the faculty at Princeton University, where he remained fifteen years. He left in 1946 to accept an appointment as a professor

10. Henry Eyring, "My Father's Formula," *Ensign* 8 (October 1978): 29. See also Edward L. Kimball, "Harvey Fletcher and Henry Eyring: Men of Faith and Science," *Dialogue: A Journal of Mormon Thought* 15 (Autumn 1982): 81.

of chemistry and dean of the Graduate School at the University of Utah. His department chair and graduate dean at Princeton declared: "One might say that Eyring possesses the Midas touch. Everything in scientific research turns to gold when brought to the attention of his fertile brain."[11] Eyring remained at the University of Utah until his death in 1981 at the age of eighty. His contributions were legion. He came to be known for his work on the causes of diseases that germinate life, and his ongoing contributions to mining, engineering, metallurgy, ceramics, fuels, explosives, plastics, fibers, and theoretical chemistry.

The Eyrings were active in the LDS Church wherever they lived. Science, Eyring always insisted, kept him humble. His faith, he said, was a simple one: "I take very seriously the idea that there is a God. It is all very real to me. When we think we see conflicts between science and religion, we must remember that these conflicts are in our own minds. There are no such conflicts in God's mind. For me, there has been no serious difficulty in reconciling the principles of true science with the principles of true religion, for both are concerned with the eternal verities of the universe."[12]

Eyring was an LDS branch president, district president, stake high councilor, and for twenty-five years a member of the church's General Sunday School Board. He had a keen intellect, Edison-like industry, perseverance, and good physical health. A great teacher, his explanations at complex chemical theories were remarkably clear. Always enthusiastic, he showed considerable energy in his lectures and research. He enjoyed talking in LDS ward sacrament meetings and stake firesides, and did not hesitate to discuss religion at scientific assemblies. He received honorary degrees from fifteen universities, and more than twenty other awards. He published a dozen books

---

11. "World Famous Scientist Celebrates," *University of Utah Review*, March 1971, 4.

12. Joseph Walker, "Man of Science, Man of Faith," *LDS Church News*, December 13, 1980, 5.

and more than 600 scientific papers. All the while, he had an irrepressible sense of humor, interest in people, and an unusual zest for life. "There are only a handful of people in the history of science throughout the world who've been so prolific," said one of his colleagues.[13] "I like to understand what molecules do," Eyring once commented, "but I also like to tell about what I know." In 1963, he was elected president of the 93,000-member American Chemical Society, and in 1965 was chosen president of the 100,000-member American Association for the Advancement of Science. Few men in LDS history have exemplified the unity of science and religion better than Eyring.[14] He had no difficulty in reconciling the principles of science with those of religion, and often said so.

Something of a stir occurred in 1953 when Joseph Fielding Smith, president of the church's Council of Twelve Apostles, published his controversial book *Man, His Origin and Destiny.* The book, based on literal interpretations of scripture, asserted that the earth's life was very short, that no human life existed on earth prior to the advent of Adam and Eve, that the biological theory of evolution was opposed to LDS scripture, and that science was antagonistic to religion. Some members of the Quorum of the Twelve were concerned that the book might be used in the Institutes of Religion as an authoritative text. Eyring, as a leading LDS scientist, was asked to write his opinion. In a lengthy and widely circulated

---

13. "Another Milestone for Eyring," *University of Utah Review,* January 1973, 4.

14. See Eyring, *The Faith of a Scientist* (Salt Lake City: Bookcraft, 1967); Steve H. Heath, "Henry Eyring, Mormon Scientist" (master's thesis, University of Utah, 1980); Mildred Bennion Eyring, *My Autobiography* (Salt Lake City: Privately published, 1969); Paul R. Green, *Science and Your Faith in God* (Salt Lake City: Bookcraft, 1958): Duane E. Jeffery, "Seers, Savants, and Evolution: The Uncomfortable Interface," *Dialogue: A Journal of Mormon Thought* 8 (Autumn–Winter 1973): 41–75; and Edward L. Kimball, "A Dialogue With Henry Eyring," *Dialogue: A Journal of Mormon Thought* 8 (Autumn–Winter 1973): 99–108. For a book-length biography, see Henry J. Eyring, *Mormon Scientist: The Life and Faith of Henry Eyring* (Salt Lake City: Deseret Book Co., 2008).

response dated December 16, 1951, Eyring gave the scientific evidence for the ancient age of the earth, defended the pro-science views of Elders James Talmage and John Widtsoe, contended that earth history is easily reconcilable to the gospel, and pointed out that the prophets, as with all of us, "must walk by faith and wait and study in order to partly understand many of God's wonderful works." It is difficult, Eyring said, "to decide what [in the scriptures] is to be taken literally and what is figurative."[15] Lowell Bennion, for one, congratulated Eyring on his position in a letter saying that Eyring's letter displayed clarity, integrity, and humility. As the result of Eyring's letter and others that followed, and personal conversations with LDS leaders, Church President David O. McKay, the First Presidency, and the Council of Twelve stated that Smith's book represented the personal views of its author and not the official position of the church.[16]

A kind of folk hero among the Saints, Eyring became an important authority on science and religion. He was also a symbol of one who had achieved academically and was still faithful. In 1961, he was featured in an LDS Church-sponsored film, *Search for Truth,* which argued that the principles of true science and true religion were in complete accord. In 1967, his book *Faith of a Scientist* appeared, copies of which were distributed in paperback to approximately 150,000 of the church's youth. Eyring's views were thus propounded with official fanfare. As Eyring expressed in a letter to N. Eldon Tanner, of the church's First Presidency, in 1967, his views may be summarized as follows:

> The gospel embraces all truth. Brigham Young especially emphasized the propriety of seeking all truth. The assumption that because a man understands something about the operation of the Universe,

15. Steven H. Heath, "The Reconciliation of Faith and Science: Henry Eyring's Achievement," *Dialogue: A Journal of Mormon Thought* 15 (Autumn 1982): 90.

16. See Jeffery, "Seers, Savants, and Evolution," 66–67.

he will necessarily be less faithful is a gratuitous assumption contradicted by numberless examples. God, who understands all about the Universe, is apparently, not troubled by this knowledge.

Some people drift when they study, but some people drift when they don't study. If the church espouses the cause of ignorance, it will alienate more people than if it advises man to seek after truth, even at some risk.[17]

Hugh Nibley

On March 31, 1985, the 75th birthday of Hugh Nibley, the Foundation for Ancient Research and Mormon Studies (FARMS) at Brigham Young University announced the completion of arrangements to publish the "Complete Collected Works of Hugh Nibley." One of the LDS Church's most prolific scholars, Nibley had published a dozen books, twenty articles in professional journals, 400 articles in church magazines, and had delivered hundreds of addresses before church and professional groups. Among the volumes subsequently published are *Old Testament and Related Studies, Enoch the Prophet, The World and the Prophets, Mormonism and Early Christianity, Lehi in the Desert: The World of the Jaredites, An Approach to the Book of Mormon, Since Cumorah, The Prophetic Book of Mormon, Approaching Zion, The Ancient State, Tinkling Cymbals and Sounding Brass, Temple and Cosmos,* and *Brother Brigham Challenges the Saints.* These and other publications represent an enduring legacy of one of the church's greatest intellectuals.[18]

Nibley was born in 1910 in Portland, Oregon, the son of Alexander and Agnes Sloan Nibley. His grandfathers were: Charles W. Nibley, a businessman and financier, Presiding Bishop of the

---

17. Eyring, Letter to Tanner, October 19, 1967, in Heath, "The Reconciliation of Faith and Science," 98.

18. See Boyd Jay Petersen, *Hugh Nibley: A Consecrated Life* (Salt Lake City: Greg Kofford Books, 2002).

church, 1907–25, and counselor in the First Presidency of Heber J. Grant, 1925–31; and Alexander Neibaur, an early Jewish convert to the LDS Church, and friend and teacher of Joseph Smith.

When Nibley was a boy, his parents moved to Glendale, in Southern California, where his father became a successful real estate developer and his mother, Rebecca Ann (Neibaur) Nibley, made their elegant home a center for artists. Because of this influence, one of Nibley's brothers became a well-known Hollywood scenarist; another was concertmaster for the BYU and Utah symphonies; still another was a concert pianist playing with many professional symphonies throughout the world. Hugh recognized that his mother pushed her children—"my mother was hell on wheels."[19] His father lost a fortune during the crash of real estate values in 1930.

As a teenager, Nibley developed an interest in languages and word origins. He studied Greek, Hebrew, Egyptian, Babylonian, Coptic, and later Sanskrit and Arabic. When he was seventeen, he was sent as an LDS missionary to Germany. The European culture allowed him to continue his study of languages amid his proselytizing and teaching. Upon his return, in 1930, he enrolled at the University of California, Los Angeles, where he majored in history and minored in Classics. After graduation, he was a research fellow at the University of California in Berkeley, 1936–37, and received a PhD from Berkeley in 1938.

Once more Nibley was sent to the LDS Swiss–German Mission, then transferred to the LDS Northwestern States Mission because of World War II. From 1942 to 1945, he was an intelligence officer with the US Army, and on D-Day in June 1944 he parachuted behind enemy lines and worked several months with the underground.[20]

---

19. "A Conversation With Hugh Nibley," *Dialogue: A Journal of Mormon Thought* 12 (Winter 1979): 12.

20. For more, see Hugh Nibley and Alex Nibley, *Sergeant Nibley, Ph.D.: Memories of an Unlikely Screaming Eagle* (Salt Lake City: Deseret Book Co., 2006).

Hugh Nibley

In 1946, at the end of the war, Nibley joined the faculty of Brigham Young University as a professor of history and philosophy. He retired in 1975, but continued teaching until 1994. He and his wife, Phyllis (Draper) Nibley (b. 1926), had eight children.

As a BYU faculty member, Nibley contributed important articles to professional journals, including *The Classical Journal, Western Political Quarterly, The Historian, Western Speech, Jewish Historical Review, Church History, BYU Studies,* and various encyclopedias. At the same time, he submitted a steady stream of articles to *The Improvement Era, The Instructor, LDS Millennial Star,* and other church publications. His LDS books included *Lehi in the Desert and the World of the Jaredites* (1952); *The World of the Prophets* (1954); *An Approach to the Book of Mormon* (1957), originally a priesthood manual; *The Mythmakers* (1961), a witty, mocking review of the writings of early critics of Joseph Smith; *Sounding Brass* (1963), a satirical commentary on Irving Wallace's book *Wife Number Twenty-Seven* about Brigham Young's tumultuous marriage to Ann Eliza Webb; *Since Cumorah* (1968), an effort to test the validity of the Book of Mormon; *The Message of the Joseph Smith Papyri: An Egyptian Endowment* (1975); and *Abraham in Egypt* (1981), a book about Joseph Smith's "Book of Abraham" (now in the *Pearl of Great Price*).[21]

Nibley wrote LDS lesson manuals, books for general readers, pamphlets, reviews, radio talks, and scathing criticisms. His knowledge of languages—he had facility in fourteen—tempted him to play on words, clarify expressions and meanings, and discuss origins. For this linguistic scholar, language was a tool that helped him understand scriptures and religious and secular history. A man of considerable erudition, he was also a man of deep faith.[22]

Nibley, the stereotypical absentminded professor, taught, spoke, and wrote so long that he, too, eventually became a folk character in LDS society. He had a large following. At age eighty-four, he taught a weekly television class on the Book of Mormon; he was a perennial "Professor of the Year" at BYU; he received an Honorary Doctor of Letters degree from BYU; he established himself so well in the minds of Latter-day Saints that when he wrote an article for *Dialogue: A Journal of Mormon Thought,* which he did a few times, the compulsory lines of identification at the bottom of the first page of the article gave up the traditional write-up, and simply stated: "Hugh Nibley is." He was a "furiously active" member of the LDS Church, but, seen also as something of an idiosyncratic, he was never a ward bishop, stake president, or held office with rank in any auxiliary.

Although hundreds declared him to be the great scholar-intellectual in the church, there were a few dissenters from this judgment. He

---

21. See Louis Midgley, "Hugh Nibley: A Short Bibliographical Note," *Dialogue: A Journal of Mormon Thought* 2 (Spring 1967): 119–21.

22. See Truman G. Madsen, "Foreword," in *Nibley on the Timely and Timeless* (Provo, Utah: BYU Religious Studies Center, 1978), xvii.

was called "an ardent apologist," and his writings were heavily enlarged with footnotes (an article in *Dialogue* had ten pages of text
and fourteen pages of small-print endnotes).[23] Indeed, he used an
overwhelming, sometimes bewildering variety of sources with care-
free gusto. In *Abraham in Egypt*, he used information from several
periods of Egyptian, Mesopotamian, Israelite, Canaanite, Greek, and
Christian history. In the first chapter of the book, for example, he
cited nineteen documents: the Shabako Stone, Book of Jubilees, Met-
ternich Stele, Lachish Letters, Book of the Dead, Ethiopian Book of
Enoch (First Enoch), Apocalypse of Abraham, Testament of Abraham, Gospel of the Twelve Apostles, Pyramid Texts of Unis, Coffin
texts, *The Iliad*, Justin Martyr's *Cohortatio ad Graecos*, Book of the
Two Ways, a text from the coffin of a daughter of Psammerichus II,
Amduat, and Genesis.[24] One reviewer suggested, "His efforts to make
the advances and dangers of philology available to the lay reader are
often insightful and always entertaining."[25] In some instances, however, Nibley's work could be unfocused and confusing. Regardless,
his knowledge and research were prodigious. He made the Book of
Mormon an exciting treasure trove for a whole generation—two generations!—of readers. Put simply, he was a great teacher.

No one, however, could accuse Nibley of taking himself too
seriously. Some of his talks were hilarious and every book and article contained funny and clever asides.[26] As Nibley himself said,
"Everything goes in a free discussion as long as the discussion is

---

23. See Nibley, "Treasures in the Heavens: Some Early Christian Insights into
the Organizing of Worlds," *Dialogue: A Journal of Mormon Thought* 8 (Autumn–
Winter 1973): 76–98.

24. See Eric Jay Olson, "The Extremes of Eclecticism," *Dialogue: A Journal of
Mormon Thought* 15 (Winter 1982): 123.

25. Ibid., 125.

26. See Nibley, "Bird Island," *Dialogue: A Journal of Mormon Thought* 10 (Autumn 1977): 120–23.

going on—give it time and everything will come out in the wash."[27] Above all, he had a contempt for academic pretension. A classic Nibley talk was "Zeal Without Knowledge," given as part of the celebration of Academic Emphasis week at BYU and later published in the Nibley volume *The Timely and The Timeless* (1978). Another classic was "Leaders to Managers: The Fatal Shift," his BYU Commencement Address on August 19, 1983.[28]

One of Nibley's admirers suggested that Nibley conducted a two-front war—against cultural Mormonism and against sectarian Mormonism. Cultural Mormons are those who may not be full believers but who respect the values of the faith—the work ethic, the honesty, the emphasis on the family. Sectarian Mormons are those who use the faith to sanctify a radical political ideology or to attach extremist interpretations.[29] The Book of Mormon does not support either position, Nibley contended in *Since Cumorah*. Neither liberal nor conservative, Nibley sought to show the relevance of the Book of Mormon to current problems—the danger of accepting leaders' opinions without thinking through the problems; the false ambitions of being overly concerned with wealth, status, and power; the tendency to call out the thought police; and the failure to recognize our obligations to the environment.

Nibley's influence was incalculable. His long career of scholarship revealed a mind and style that were lively and vigorous, that scholarly oriented writing could exhibit both faith and intellect, that the essential themes of Mormonism exhibited an ancient context, and that Joseph Smith was, as Nibley wrote, "a colossus of authentic insight."

Nibley passed away in 2005 in his Provo home. He was 94 years old.

---

27. Ibid., 123.

28. *Dialogue: A Journal of Mormon Thought* 16 (Winter 1983): 12–21.

29. Louis C. Midgley, "The Secular Relevance of the Gospel," *Dialogue: A Journal of Mormon Thought* 4 (Winter 1969): 76–85.

All three men profiled in this chapter, Bennion, Eyring, and Nibley, made remarkable contributions to the ability to think critically as individuals and to feel the power of the LDS gospel. They were singular in their areas of achievement, with brilliant intellects and steadfast faith.

CHAPTER 7

Chieko Okazaki, Laurel Thatcher Ulrich, and Claudia Lauper Bushman

EDUCATORS AND HUMANISTS

Religious leaders teach by persuasion, by example, by logic, by imaginative reason, or by the recitation of scripture. According to the Gospels, Jesus, the master teacher, spent part of his public life teaching through stories. The Gospel writer Mark even went so far as to declare that all of Jesus' words were parables (4:34)—that is, metaphoric narratives and aphorisms intended for instruction and edification. Biblical scholar John Dominic Crossan lists twenty-six separate parables related by Jesus in the Gospels of Matthew, Mark, and Luke.[1]

Early Christian history, whether oral or written, consisted primarily of stories, testimonies, and narratives of personal experience about Jesus and his disciples. The theology came later. But a contrary influence lessened its prominent sway. The Greek culture that surrounded them emphasized argument and rational thinking. By subjecting myths, legends, tales, allegories, and fables to critical scrutiny, Greek thinkers tended to relegate storytelling and testimony to a lesser place. Although narrative and testimony remained in Christian literature, the pervading influence of Greek philosophers was strong.[2]

---

1. In Paul J. Achtemeier, ed., *Harper's Bible Dictionary* (San Francisco: Harper & Row, 1985), 748.

2. Scholars sometimes use myth as a synonym for story. Some people recoil at the term myth as being something "made up," fictional, not true. Actually, it is a technical term used by scholars to mean a story, presented as having actually

Another influence that tended to discourage the creative re-telling of stories was the concept of the closed canon. The core of God's message to humankind, some thought, ended with the Old and New Testaments. No retelling or further telling of stories in accordance with the contemporary situation was encouraged. There are exceptions, such as St. Francis of Assisi, but there was a tendency for repetition of scripture to replace creative adaptation of the gospel spirit in stories and metaphors appropriate to the contemporary scene. Yet, as Nigerian writer Chinua Achebe observed in his 1987 novel *Anthills of Savannah*, "The story is our escort; without it, we are blind."[3]

What a glorious thing for the Latter-day Saints when Joseph Smith reopened the canon of scripture, recorded his stories of visions and revelations, reemphasized testimony, and revived the practice of storytelling. As a community of storytellers, the early Saints read accounts of conversions and spiritual encounters in tracts and such early magazines as *Messenger and Advocate, Elder's Journal, Times and Seasons,* and the *Millennial Star.* In pioneer Utah, they could read them in the *Deseret News Weekly, Journal of Discourses, Juvenile Instructor, The Contributor, Woman's Exponent, Young Woman's Journal,* and the *Faith Promoting Series* of "little" books published by the Juvenile Instructor Office and George Q. Cannon & Sons Printers. These included stories from the Bible, Book of Mormon, early LDS Church history, individual diaries and family histories, and from personal recollections. The stories were an attempt to convey

---

occurred in a previous age, explaining the cosmological and supernatural traditions of a people—their gods, heroes, cultural traits, and religious beliefs. Robert. A. Oden Jr., "Myth and Mythology," in *Anchor Bible Dictionary,* eds. David Noel Freedman et al., 6 Vols. (New York: Doubleday, 1992), 4:948. Myths provide intellectually satisfying explanations of many questions about the purpose of life, the behavior of the universe, and the nature of the divine. Nothing disrespectful or disbelieving is intended by referring to a sacred doctrine like the resurrection of the Savior as a myth.

3. Qtd. in Bernth Lindfors, ed., *Conversations with Chinua Achebe,* (Jackson: University Press of Mississippi, 1997), xi.

the richness and connectedness of Smith's and others' experiences with the divine. The individual stories and testimonies gave human warmth and actuality to the historical generalizations of the historians. As events were turned into stories and testimonies, the pioneer Saints were motivated to set themselves right with God. Their faith was strengthened, and, in a world of conflict and confusion, they accepted "the truth" and gathered to Zion. They became "doers of the word" (James 1:22).

A master storyteller in LDS history was church general authority J. Golden Kimball (1853–1938). Even today, his colorful stories instruct, inspire, and entertain. They are relevant to our lives and interests. Listening to gospel stories and to the recitation of sacred experiences—in Sunday sacrament meetings, in worldwide general conference, in local firesides—enhances our experience of life and salvation. Discursive argument has its place, "objective" history has its place, but I do not believe that a factual basis is a requirement for a narrative to speak to us or to move us.

As children of God, we benefit from both reason and poetry, reason and imagination, reason and religion. If reason helps us to think objectively, sacred stories and poems enable us to utilize and exhibit the power of subjective feeling of the invisible truths of life.

Sacred stories, both ancient and modern, help us to understand why we are here and what we must do, and give concrete expression to the doctrines taught by Amos, Ezekiel, Jesus, Joseph Smith, Brigham Young, and our own ancestors and parents. They describe the reality of transcendental experiences, interpret and give meaning to historical events, designate the ongoing significance of persons and events for subsequent generations. This may be what Church President Spencer W. Kimball meant when he told the students and faculty of Brigham Young University in his "Second Century Address" (1975) that they must be "bilingual." "As LDS scholars," he said, "you must speak with authority and excellence to your professional colleagues in the language of scholarship; and you must also be literate in the language of spiritual things."[4]

Chieko Okazaki

An example of the tradition of storytelling and sermonizing in the late twentieth-century LDS Church is Hawaiian native Chieko Okazaki, who served as First Counselor in the general presidency of the Relief Society from 1990 to 1997. The daughter of agricultural plantation laborers, Chieko Nishimura was born in 1926 in Kohala, on the northern end of the big island of Hawaii. As a child, she learned to read the sea, to know if the tide was coming in or going out, if it was safe to swim, and when the angle of the sun meant she must return home. She watched and learned from people. She grew up among a handful of Japanese families in a village that was part Japanese and part Hawaiian. The children grew up speaking a combination of Japanese, English, and Hawaiian. The family had no radio, no books or magazines. In school, she struggled to learn to read in English. She had a good visual memory and memorized "Run, Spot, run," and other words in books she was given to read. Her teacher read stories about Jack and the beanstalk and Little Red Riding Hood, which she enjoyed, but she was not able to visualize a beanstalk or a wolf. Unfortunately, there were no stories about coconut palms or mongooses.[5]

In the third grade, Chieko enjoyed reading *Aesop's Fables* and in the fifth grade Jack London's *Call of the Wild*. The experience was all the more difficult because she had to open and hold American books differently than Japanese books, and move her eyes in a different direction while reading. She studied hard and wanted to

---

4. *BYU Studies* 16 (Summer 1976): 446.

5. Based upon an address Okazaki gave on April 9, 1994, at the Women's Week at Utah Valley Community College (later Utah Valley University), a copy of which she supplied to me and gave me permission to use.

Chieko Okazaki

understand the world of the *haoles*. Even much later, she preferred to thresh out ideas in conversation rather than on paper. This is one reason, perhaps, that this child of Hawaii became a notable teacher and sermonizer. Her teachers, she said, made deep impressions on her; they were people who learned all the time.

Raised as a Buddhist, Chieko joined the LDS Church in 1942, at age fifteen. From Buddhism, she learned about prayer, righteousness, service to others, honoring parents, and doing her best. When hands were laid upon her head after her LDS baptism and she received the gift of the Holy Ghost, however, she was a heartfelt-converted Christian. She felt the presence of Jesus, had his help in making decisions, was comforted in her sadness, and experienced joy in her successes. As long as she was faithful, Jesus was with her, whether she was walking on the beach of Mahukona or the sidewalks of Honolulu. She felt the Spirit strongly when she attended church meetings, and the Spirit remained with her when she went home, out into the field, or into the classroom.[6]

One reason she related so readily to Christ when she was a teenager was, as she later explained, "because what he was teaching was clear, and what he did made sense. In fact, it seemed like exactly what I was taught at home."[7]

Chieko married Edward Y. Okazaki (1923–92) on Maui in 1949 when the two were fellow students attending the University of Hawaii. Two years later, they were sealed for time and eternity in the LDS Honolulu temple. Sister Okazaki earned a bachelor's degree and a fifth-year degree in education from the University of Hawaii, a master's degree in education from the University of Northern Colorado, and a doctorate in educational administration from Colorado State University. She taught elementary school in Hawaii, Salt Lake City, and Denver. She also worked ten years as an elementary school principal in Denver.

Okazaki was called to the LDS Church's Young Women General Board in 1961 (serving to 1966), the first non-Caucasian to serve on any of the church's general boards. She had been stake Young Women president and ward Relief Society president. She later served on the Primary General Board of the church (1988–90). From 1968 to 1971, she served with her husband when he was called to open the church's Japan–Okinawa Mission.

Okazaki grappled with intellectual problems by what might be called homiletical theology. Her talks and writings focused on the Bible, Book of Mormon, Doctrine and Covenants, and the writings of LDS Church leaders; the use of experience to teach faith and faith to teach experience; the possibility of exaltation by living the principles and participating in ordinances; the selection of words

---

6. Okazaki, "I Will Never Leave You," in *Cat's Cradle* (Salt Lake City: Bookcraft, 1993), 176–77.

7. Okazaki address of April 9, 1994, 4.

that are meaningful and persuasive and not just informational; an emphasis on maintaining healthy relationships with others and with God; and an awareness of the needs of others for spiritual, emotional, and intellectual nourishment.

Okazaki's two books, both published in 1993–94, are examples of the combination of faith and intellect—with an international perspective. She was a master of taking the simple experiences of life and extracting lessons for all to learn. *Lighten Up!*, a quotation from the ancient "Book of Okazaki," Chapter 1 verse 1, is a cheerful invitation to enjoy the gospel, celebrate human diversity, increase charity, and serve enthusiastically. "Walk in My Zori"—the equivalent of "walk in my moccasins"—recounts lessons she learned from the sacrifices her family made for her education. Story after story gives suggestions for parenting and for freeing one's life from guilt, prejudice, and unrealistic expectations. Her personal experiences, told with warmth and affection, offer insights into life, help to induce partnership in marriage and church callings, to tell of the process and joy of service, and to teach us how to accept and handle our mistakes. Her stories are poignant, humorous, encouraging, and profound.[8]

Her second book, *Cat's Cradle,* takes its name from an ordinary piece of string that evolves into a pattern, showing the interconnectedness and intersections of our lives and how we can adapt this pattern in our marriages, church callings, responses to adversity, and opportunities to serve. Her sermons, given in prose that is lucid and occasionally stunning, are a testimony to her faith, to the power and beauty of the language of faith, and to the effectiveness of language and experience for personal nurture. People in her audiences put aside their concerns and found themselves simply loving to listen.

Okazaki died in Salt Lake City in 2011. She was eighty-four.

---

8. In January 1994, Okazaki was given a special citation from the Association for Mormon Letters for literary excellence for her *Lighten Up!*

Laurel Thatcher Ulrich

Other distinguished women demonstrated this combination of faith and intellect and practiced homiletical theology. Two of these women are Laurel Thatcher Ulrich and Claudia Lauper Bushman.

Laurel was born in 1938 in St. Anthony, Idaho, but grew up in Sugar City, Idaho, where her father, John Kenneth Thatcher, was principal and later superintendent of schools. Her father was a grandson of early LDS converts in Virginia who migrated to Utah and settled in Logan, Cache Valley, Utah. Her great-grandfather, John B. Thatcher, an early Idaho settler, gave Thatcher, Idaho, its name, while her father was a state senator from Madison County, Idaho, and member of the Idaho State Board of Education.

Laurel graduated from Sugar–Salem High School, then from the University of Utah with a major in literature, and after marriage to Gael Ulrich completed a doctorate in history at the University of New Hampshire where her husband was a professor of chemical engineering. The pair were always active in their local LDS ward; Gael was bishop, stake high councilor, and counselor in another bishopric; Laurel was Primary, Sunday school, Young Women, and Relief Society teacher, and taught LDS seminary. They have five children.

While caring for her husband and children, working for university degrees, and serving one or two positions in her LDS ward, Ulrich was one of the founders of *Exponent II,* a quarterly magazine by and for LDS women. She wrote articles for almost every issue, which related personal experiences and impressions on such topics as large families, "Counseling the Brethren," stake high council talks, Young Women's programs, sacrament meetings, Relief Society activities, feminism, and the LDS priesthood.

Ulrich also contributed several articles to *Dialogue: A Journal of Mormon Thought,* all written with spiritual conviction and technical skill. As part of a Relief Society fundraising project, joined by other women in their ward, she wrote *A Beginner's Boston* (published by

Laurel Thatcher Ulrich

the LDS Cambridge, Massachusetts, Ward Relief Society in 1966 and 1967), which went through two editions and three printings. As part of another Relief Society fundraising project, she (and Dell Fox who drew the illustrations) rhymed the humorous *L is for Indian: An Alphabet for Little Saints* (1972), proposing that D is for deacon, F is for fast day, I is for iron rod, K is for Kolob, and so on.

In the early 1970s, some of the women who had published *Beginner's Boston* began researching the lives of early LDS women for a series of lessons for an LDS Institute of Religion class entitled "Roots and Fruits of Mormon Women." At Radcliffe College's Schlesinger Library, one of the women discovered a complete set of the LDS women's newspaper *Woman's Exponent,* a bi-monthly by and for LDS women edited by Emmeline B. Wells and published in Salt Lake City from 1872 to 1914. Ulrich and her Relief Society sisters spent months reading to each other from the papers.

The activity inspired the women to take seriously the lives of other women, and so was born *Exponent II*, a newspaper by and about contemporary LDS women. Also in the early 1970s, the group formed Emmeline Press and published their LDS Institute lessons about women in early Utah as chapters in a book titled *Mormon Sisters: Women in Early Utah.*

These group efforts motivated Ulrich to continue her own research, and in 1980, after five part-time years working on a master's degree and nine years on a doctorate, she received a PhD in history from the University of New Hampshire at Durham. Her book, published in 1982, was *Good Wives: Image and Reality in the Lives of Women in Northern New England, 1650–1750.* The book was well reviewed. Not quite a decade later, she published *A Midwife's Tale: The Life of Martha Ballard Based on Her Diary, 1785–1812,* which won the Bancroft and John H. Dunning Awards of the American Historical Association, the Joan Kelly Memorial Prize in Women's History of the Organization of American Historians, and the Pulitzer Prize for American History. She is the second Latter-day Saint to win the Pulitzer Prize for history.

A Midwife's Tale was praised for its imaginative use of the Ballard diary to recreate life on the early American frontier. Ulrich's interpretation of the data "discloses the operation of a female economy, reveals the importance of the midwife in the life of a rural community, and provides insight into gender roles and relationships." It is a work of scholarship and art, a Latter-day Saint woman's important effort to make the women (and men) of early New England come to life. Using Ballard's long-neglected diary as the basis of her study, Ulrich pieced together a fascinating account of women's lives and work in pre-industrial America. Employing a variety of sources ranging from wills, tax lists, deeds, court records, and town meeting minutes to medical treatises, novels, religious tracts, and the papers of Maine physicians, she informs readers of early American courtship, marriage practices, and sexual mores as well as of quilting bees, weaving, gardening, and tending to livestock. There are perceptive comments about family relations, rape, incest, premarital sex, illegitimacy, and even murder and suicide. Ballard, readers learn, was midwife, nurse, physician, mortician, pharmacist, and attentive wife as well as a keeper of vital records of her town.[9] Colonial women, their work, their suffering and joy, their myths and legends, come vibrantly alive in *A Midwife's Tale*. It was and remains "a literary masterpiece, crafted and full of sentient impact."[10]

For *A Midwife's Tale* and other work, Ulrich received two honors never previously awarded to a Latter-day Saint: The John D. and Catherine T. MacArthur Award of $365,000 (sometimes referred to as a genius award) to encourage creativity, no strings attached, to support her for five years as she researched, wrote, traveled, and lectured in the years to come; and the Charles Frankel Award of the National Humanities Commission for brilliance in historical writing. She was also awarded in 1992 an honorary doctor of humane letters from the University of Utah in a ceremony at which she was also the commencement speaker. In 2007, she published *Well-Behaved Women Seldom Make History*. From 2008 to 2009, she was president of the American Historical Association; and from 2014 to 2015 she was president of the Mormon History Association. And in 2017, she published *A House Full of Females: Plural Marriage and Women's Rights in Early Mormonism, 1835–1870*.

In her 1992 commencement address, Ulrich detailed her life of the past thirty-two years (she had graduated from the University of

---

9. See the review of *A Midwife's Tale* by Judy Barrett Litoff in *American Historical Review* (June 1991): 950–51.

10. Gene Sessions's review in *Dialogue: A Journal of Mormon Thought* 16 (Winter 1983): 149–51.

Utah in 1960), explaining how she came to blend a life of mother-hood and scholarship:

> I am grateful that 32 years ago I earned both a Phi Beta Kappa
> Key and a safety pin, and that for the past twenty years I have
> been able to combine motherhood with "a practical life work."
> My children's lives have been enriched by my scholarship, and
> my scholarship has been enriched by my life as a housewife and
> mother. When people ask me how I have done it, I usually say, "A
> little at a time."[11]

Claudia Lauper Bushman

Claudia Lauper was born in 1934 in San Francisco, the granddaugh-ter of LDS converts from four countries who immigrated to Utah in the nineteenth century, and the daughter of a father who was, in succession, an LDS ward bishop, stake president, temple worker, and stake patriarch, and a mother who was interested in music. She is the youngest of four daughters. Both of her grandfathers were farmers who did not do well in Utah. They eventually migrated to California, part of the great emigration from Utah in the 1920s and 1930s that carried Mormonism to urban centers in California. Her father and his brother were among the first to seek their fortunes in the West. After her father served an LDS proselytizing mission in the Southern States—a companion for a while of my father, who was called from his farm in Idaho in the mid-1920s, leaving behind my mother and five children—he returned to San Francisco, where he was successful in business, church, and community.

Claudia and her sisters were always active in the LDS Church, participated in dances, plays, musicals, Mutual Improvement Asso-ciation functions, and gave Sunday sacrament meeting talks. They did well in school and had many friends. Upon graduation from

---

11. See *Exponent II* 17 (1992): 19.

Claudia Lauper Bushman

high school, Claudia received a scholarship to Wellesley College in Wellesley, Massachusetts. There she majored in English literature and earned a BA degree. Every Sunday, she went to church meetings in Cambridge, Massachusetts, and thus became acquainted with many Latter-day Saints in the Boston area, some of them transfers from Utah, Idaho, and California. In her junior year, she married Richard Lyman Bushman (b. 1931), a native of Utah who had filled an LDS mission in New England and was beginning graduate studies in history at Harvard. Claudia completed her studies at Wellesley and was wearing a maternity dress under her graduation gown when she received her degree.

Bushman, who believed strongly that a married woman should be first of all a good wife and second a good mother to her children, also believed in Joseph Smith's revelations that women should magnify their own callings and enlarge the minds and talents—for their own benefit and for the benefit of society. When her husband accepted his first teaching position at Brigham Young University, she determined that, along with having babies and looking after them and fulfilling a church calling in the Primary, she would take a graduate class or two every semester at the university with the help of her husband, his mother, and others. In three years, she bore her third child and earned an MA degree from BYU in American Literature.

In 1963, when Richard accepted a two-year fellowship at Brown University in Providence, Rhode Island, Claudia helped with family finances by teaching two freshman English classes at Rhode Island College before she retired to have her fourth child. Back at BYU, she taught freshman English again. When she told her department chair that she expected child number five, he told her she would have to quit teaching.

During this year, Richard won the prestigious Bancroft Prize for his first book, *From Puritan to Yankee,* completed a fellowship at Harvard, and was offered a professorship in American Studies at Boston University. In addition to her motherly duties—feeding babies, changing diapers, preparing meals, folding laundry, settling squabbles, getting the children dressed for church, helping the older ones with homework, baking cookies for parties, taking them to dance and music lessons, and helping them prepare talks for church—Claudia entertained guests and attended school and church ceremonies with Richard, accepted assignments in her local Primary and Relief Society, was "Mrs. Bishop" of their Cambridge, Massachusetts, ward, and began a doctoral program in American Studies at Boston University.

In 1978, after fourteen years and another baby, for a total of six, Bushman completed the PhD qualifying her for professional positions that would thereafter fit into her personal, church, and family life.

When Richard was sustained as president of the LDS Boston

Stake, and some people thought Claudia's editorship of *Exponent II* was unsuitable for the wife of a stake president, she resigned from the publication. Others thought the publication was definitely helpful for LDS women, and the paper has continued to this day.

A year or two later, Richard was recruited by the University of Delaware, and decided to make the change. Because he was made chair of the history department, this meant that Claudia would never be hired to teach history at the university. She completed her dissertation, which was later published as *"A Good Poor Man's Wife": Being a Chronicle of Harriet Hanson Robinson and Her Family in Nineteenth-Century New England* (1981). This was a study of a middle-class housewife and mother who overcame various difficulties to gain an education, work in various reform efforts, and write several books. Reviewers regarded the book as an important contribution to women's studies, family history, and American history.

Since Bushman was not permitted to teach history courses at Delaware, she taught classes in other departments, mostly in the honors program—courses in women's studies, history, and literature. There she experienced the discrimination that many of my generation suffered from: the women's history department refused to cross-list her honor's program classes because she was LDS. She gave up doing women's history, and instead became a local historian. She taught Delaware history, did a history of her town Newark, organized the Newark Historical Society, and sponsored many public meetings, events, and publications.

During this period, she and other members of their LDS Elkton, Maryland, Ward, over which Richard served as bishop, began work on "The Record Year," an effort to document one calendar year in a contemporary LDS ward. They taped meetings, took pictures, collected handouts, wrote up activities, and interviewed and transcribed interviews with more than one hundred ward members, active and inactive. The papers are deposited in the archives at Brigham Young

University, and were also used to create the informative book *Mormon Lives: A Year in Elkton Ward,* by Susan Buhler Taber (1993).

Mormon Lives offers what may be the most honest, engaging, and authentic look available on contemporary Mormonism. At the heart of the book are the oral histories, each giving the story of one person's life in the church. The experiences are unquestionably diverse, furnishing telling evidence of the tension between "revealed truth" and human experience. Members' lives and everyday miracles are real, and show readers how much can be learned and how faith can be kept alive by sharing faith-affirming stories and experiences. Bushman was director of the ward choir, and her personal story is particularly poignant as she describes how she enjoyed expressing her personal faith through music.

Meanwhile, Claudia was employed to supervise the Delaware Heritage Commission, a state agency. They staged important events, arranged for the introduction of two US commemorative postage stamps that featured Delaware, and published a shelf full of books, including three by Bushman herself.

When Richard was offered a chair in early America history at Columbia University in 1990, the Bushmans moved to New York City. Claudia's first project there, as part of the 500th anniversary of the voyage of Christopher Columbus, was the publication of *America Discovers Columbus: How an Italian Explorer Became an American Hero* (1992). The book received positive reviews, and gave Claudia some good connections and opportunities. Claudia's subsequent books include *Contemporary Mormonism: Latter-day Saints in Modern America* (2006) and, with her husband, *Building the Kingdom: A History of Mormonism in America* (2001). In addition, Claudia has published important articles on LDS topics in *Dialogue: A Journal of Mormon Thought* and in *Exponent II.*[12]

---

12. See the study of the LDS Sunset Ward Chapel in *Dialogue: A Journal of Mormon Thought* 22 (Summer 1989): 119–30; "Light and Dark Thoughts on Death,"

Okazaki, Ulrich, and Bushman have all helped LDS women and men better appreciate and understand the events, personalities, and issues of the past and the present, and to cultivate a closer relationship with our heavenly parents.[13]

Dialogue: A Journal of Mormon Thought 14 (Winter 1981): 169–77; and "A Celebration of Sisterhood," *Dialogue: A Journal of Mormon Thought* 20 (Summer 1987): 128–35.

13. In addition to those mentioned, other books in which LDS women have expressed themselves on religious topics include Mary Lythgoe Bradford, ed., *Mormon Women Speak: A Collection of Essays* (Salt Lake City: Olympus Publishing Company, 1982); Maureen Ursenbach Beecher and Lavina Fielding Anderson, eds., *Sisters in Spirit: Mormon Women in Historical and Cultural Perspective* (Urbana: University of Illinois Press, 1987); and Maxine Hanks, ed., *Women and Authority: Re-emerging Mormon Feminism* (Salt Lake City: Signature Books, 1992).

Conclusion

Of the several leaders of LDS thought mentioned in the previous chapters, two were presidents of the church, one was a member of the church's First Presidency, two were general officers of the Relief Society, one was a president of the First Quorum of Seventy, two were educators, and one was a scientist. Some, as in the case of Joseph Smith, were young. Some sermonized, lectured, and wrote about Mormonism all their lives. J. Reuben Clark's influence extended from the time he was sustained to the First Presidency in 1933 until his death in 1961 at age ninety.

All had different temperaments: Joseph Smith was creative and full of passion for the gospel. Brigham Young was an organizer and administrator, not without fervor but strongly influenced by Smith. Emmeline B. Wells and B. H. Roberts were intelligent, imaginative, and prodigious writers; they read widely, and had a broad inclusive influence. J. Reuben Clark was conservative in his viewpoints, Roberts and Lowell Bennion more liberal. Henry Eyring was a staunch advocate of the harmony of scientific truth with the gospel, and Hugh Nibley was an equally resolute contender that LDS claims and beliefs are substantiated by the study of ancient texts.

The individuals mentioned in these chapters, gifted with intelligence and endowed by the Spirit with faith, articulated LDS religious experience and spiritual aspiration. Each enjoyed the blessings of heaven, the inspiration of the scriptures, the sermons of associates and authorities, and the instructions given in general conferences, Sunday school classes, and ward priesthood and Relief Society meetings. These provided sounding boards, mental stimulation, and spiritual quickening.

In recent years, a continuing and in some ways healthy tension has existed between what might be called conservatives and liberals in the church. In an imaginative, if also somewhat simplistic, use of LDS symbolism, Richard D. Poll (1918–94), at the time a professor of history at Brigham Young University, suggested that these might be referred to as "Iron Rod Saints" and "Liahona Saints."[1] Both terms come from the Book of Mormon. The Iron Rod was the word of God; persons who clutched it could follow the straight and narrow path to the fruitful tree of life. The Liahona was a guiding compass—it did not fully mark the way, and the clarity of its directions varied with the circumstances of the user. Thus, Iron Rod Saints seek answers to their questions, both large and small, in scripture, the works of prophetic authority, official pronouncements, and the Holy Spirit. Revelation, both past and present, is the iron rod that leads persons to exaltation in the Kingdom of God. Liahona Saints may be more skeptical of some of the answers Iron Rod Saints find in their sources. No human instrument, Liahona Saints feel, is always capable of transmitting the word of God so clearly and comprehensively that it can be universally understood and easily applied. Individual human consideration is both necessary and desirable to identify the specific path we must follow. This earth was clearly defined as a test for both body and soul. Iron Rodders and Liahonas include "good" Latter-day Saints—deeply committed, living the standards, and active in their wards and stakes.

Iron Rod and Liahona Saints are among those mentioned in the preceding chapters. That these two broad types of church members have functioned as leaders of thought and action is evidence, I believe,

---

1. Poll, "What the Church Means to People Like Me," *Dialogue: A Journal of Mormon Thought* 2 (Winter 1967): 107–17.

of the church's vitality and vigor. Unlike fundamentalists in some faiths, conservative Latter-day Saints include highly educated persons who emphasize strong reliance on the wording of scripture, the authoritative structure of church government, and a church-centered social system. Liberals tend to emphasize the boldness and innovative character of Joseph Smith's Restoration, faith in the essential goodness of women and men and their possibilities of eternal progression, and the church's commitment to education and the emphasis on rationality. The checks and balances inherent in the two traditions and types of membership give Mormonism stability and progressivism.

All of the persons treated in this book were—and in the cases of Laurel Thatcher Ulrich and Claudia Lauper Bushman are—believers: valiant women and men who devoted, in varying ways, most of their lives to the gospel. The LDS Church meant everything to them. They gave up much for it, and at no time doubted seriously that it was worth it.

Joseph Smith, Brigham Young, B. H. Roberts, J. Reuben Clark, and Chieko Okazaki were born into very poor families, and, with the exceptions of Clark and Okazaki, had little formal education and were self-taught. Okazaki, Emmeline Wells, and Clark and his contemporaries had the advantage of excellent schooling. All were gifted speakers, whether of sermons or small-group lectures. At least one, Roberts, might be classified as a skilled orator. The most persuasive "fireside speakers" were of recent vintage: Bennion, Eyring, Nibley, and Okazaki.

What made these Latter-day Saints so effective was their ability to lift people out of their private and familial preoccupations and carry them beyond the personal and organizational conflicts tearing at their private lives. They prompted the pursuit of objectives worthy of their noblest efforts.

Although all possessed faith, one might speculate as to what might have happened if nothing extraordinary had happened to Joseph

Smith. He might have been a leader in New York politics. Brigham Young might have spent the rest of his life as a cabinetmaker and painter and leader in his Methodist congregation. Emmeline Wells might have been a woman of letters in Massachusetts. Restrained by British class boundaries, B. H. Roberts might have moved about from job to job and ended as an organizer for working men and women. Reuben Clark might have been retired as a senior employee of the US State Department, while Chieko Okazaki might have continued her career as a school administrator. Instead, their contributions to the LDS Church and its ongoing mission distinguished them, utilized their well-tuned talents, and assisted in building God's kingdom. These leaders demonstrate the recognition and affirmation of diversity in the LDS Church.

For believing Latter-day Saints, what holds the church together is the New and Everlasting Covenant—the restored gospel—whereby the Saints enjoy God's blessings as they work and pray for their salvation and eternal life. The scriptures and the experiences of those discussed in the foregoing chapters suggest, I strongly believe, that a combination of faith and intellect is among the means of exalting all of us.

Leonard J. Arrington (PhD, University of North Carolina) was the official Church Historian of the Church of Jesus Christ of Latter-day Saints from 1972 to 1982. During these years, he was also the director of the Charles Redd Center for Western Studies and the Lemuel H. Redd Jr. Professor of Western History at Brigham Young University (Provo, Utah). Arrington died in 1999 at age eighty-one.

Philip L. Barlow (ThD, Harvard Divinity School) was the Leonard J. Arrington Chair of Mormon History and Culture at Utah State University (Logan) from 2007 to 2018. He is currently associate director of the Neal A. Maxwell Institute for Religious Scholarship at Brigham Young University, where he is also Neal A. Maxwell Research Associate.

Gary James Bergera is managing director of the Smith–Pettit Foundation, Salt Lake City, and editor of *Confessions of a Mormon Historian: The Diaries of Leonard J. Arrington, 1971–1997,* three volumes (Signature Books).